I0957507

The Kitchen-Table Investor

JOHN F. WASIK

The Kitchen-Table
Investor

Low-Risk, Low-Maintenance
Wealth-Building
Strategies for Working Families

An Owl Book
Henry Holt and Company · New York

Henry Holt and Company, LLC
Publishers since 1866
115 West 18th Street
New York, New York 10011
Henry Holt® is a registered trademark of
Henry Holt and Company, LLC.

Distributed in Canada by H. B. Fenn and Company Ltd.

Library of Congress Cataloging-in-Publication Data
Wasik, John F.
The kitchen-table investor: low-risk, low-maintenance wealth-building
strategies for working families/
John F. Wasik.—1st ed.
p. cm.
Includes bibliographical references and index.
ISBN 0-8050-6623-3 (pb)
1. Finance, Personal. 2. Investments. I. Title.
HG179.W3192   2001
332.6—dc21   00-063228

Henry Holt books are available for special promotions and
premiums. For details contact: Director, Special Markets.

First Edition 2001

Printed in the United States of America
3   5   7   9   10   8   6   4

Contents

Preface

We can do no great things; only small things with great love.
—Mother Teresa

There's a good reason why money is likened to bread. Seemingly alive as yeast, money is inanimate, yet as if it were sustenance, we ascribe vital power to it; we certainly can't live very well without it. It is not difficult to understand how it leavens our lives, although too many people make it into one of the great mysteries of life.

As in baking bread, with money you can build an entire meal around a small amount of ingredients. The yeast for making money is very much alive and already in your mind, but you may not know it. The ingredients are sitting in your kitchen somewhere.

The truth is we're all bakers when it comes to money. It's possible to make small sums of money rise over time and become millionaires. This is not a myth. It works for millions; however, you won't find it advertised in the *Wall Street Journal,* on Internet browsers, or mentioned on any talk show. All you have to do is sit down at your kitchen table—the place where many folks talk about family finances and write their checks—and start a plan that's as automatic as buying food.

If you're one of the 20 million people who don't presently own stocks—or have just a handful of investments—and haven't saved much for retirement, this book details how to buy stocks and mutual funds at very low cost over time and build a substantial nest egg.

My low-risk, long-term strategy makes it possible for *any* investor to share in the great wealth Wall Street is producing—by investing as little as $25 a month. You'll meet people who have invested successfully without online computer trading accounts, MBAs, inherited wealth, or Ivy League degrees.

By following a handful of rules, real wealth is certainly attainable even if you don't *have* the money to invest. I'll not only show you how to invest small sums of money but help you find the money to invest *automatically* on a regular basis.

You don't have to be aggressive to win with these strategies, which are based on a proven combination of consistent investment, long-term growth, and compound interest, which any investor at any income level can employ over time. Not only does this approach work without fail, it works consistently for anybody, namely:

- If you have little disposable income
- If you don't have a generous pension or have none at all
- If you can invest only small monthly sums

Not only will this book tell you how to make a lot of money by investing relatively small amounts of money over time, but you can do so without paying a broker or middleman of any kind. And you won't need any specialized education to know how to do this. I'll even do much of the math for you to show you how it works.

More important, this strategy is not about making money for the sake of making money. It involves integrating saving and investing for a "New Prosperity," that is, a new life that will give you more time to experience its many joys. I'm building upon ideas I've developed in my three previous books on investing: *Retire Early—and Live the Life You Want Now* (Henry Holt, 2000), *The Late-Start Investor* (Henry Holt, 1999), and *The Investment Club Book* (Warner, 1995). I'll help you find your New Prosperity by creating sound personal relationships among spending, savings, and work. This is what I call a healthy *personal ecology*, or a sustainable balance between money, work, and the rest of your life. As a result, this new balance will help to (in the words of philosopher Henryk Skolimowski) "compassionately unite ourselves with the larger flow of life."

Acknowledgments

My heartfelt appreciation goes to the many people who contributed to this book. Genuine thanks goes to everyone who was interviewed, including Robin Gagliardi, her famous father, Marc Eisenson, and Nancy Castleman, his also famous partner.

To my many friends in Pittsburgh, notably Barb Lockwood, Linda Grubic, Dale Larson, Ed Thornblade, and Dave Bigley (Laurel Investment Club).

The 10-Buck club of Morgantown, West Virginia, especially Gerald Egan and Steve Sanetrik, lent their many years of club wisdom.

Eileen Matteson of the Outlook Investment Club in Littleton, Colorado, showed me the power of intergenerational investing.

Gary Mier of the WINvest club was instrumental in bringing club investing to the Internet.

Bertha Kreps of the RA club in Wisconsin defined for me the idea of taking risks at any age.

Quentin Sampson of Joliet, Illinois, was instrumental in giving me a powerful educational perspective on investing.

Special thanks to my editor, David Sobel, with whom I am reunited after a hiatus of fourteen years; my publisher, John Sterling; and my agent and friend, Robert Shepard.

Most of all, I'd like to thank the Wall Street Prowlers, which is my family's investment club. That consists of Joe and Theresa Conlon, my beloved father- and mother-in-law; Martin Conlon, my hard-working brother-in-law; Steve Beicos, a dear friend; and my talented, beautiful, and intelligent wife, Kathleen. More important, the club was *her* idea, so I can also say she is my muse in investment clubbing.

With regard to investment clubs, I am indebted to all my friends connected with the National Association of Investors Corporation.

Also thanks to my divine daughter, Sarah Virginia, whose job was cheerfully going to bed when club meetings started.

The book would not have been fully realized without the generous and loving lifelong contributions of my father, Arthur, a saver *extraordinaire,* and my mother, Virginia, to whom this book is dedicated.

—J. F. Wasik

The Kitchen-Table Investor

CHAPTER 1

Introduction: A New Prosperity Begins at the Kitchen Table

Go now and then for a fresh life—if most of humanity must go through this town stage of development—just as divers hold their breath and come ever anon to the surface to breathe. Go whether or not you have faith. Form parties, if you must be social, go to the snow-flowers in winter, to the sun-flowers in summer. Anyway, go up and away for life; be fleet!

—John Muir

It is a sultry May day in Chicago. My coworkers at *Consumers Digest* magazine are collecting money for a record $325 million, seven-state lottery payout. It is the biggest state-lottery prize ever awarded. Nobody gives a hoot about the stock market on this vernal day, and for good reason. The Dow Jones 30 Industrial Average is off 1,000 points from its high; the NASDAQ index is down 25%. The lottery mania, however, strikes me as a social ill and I inveigh against it, extolling the virtues of long-term stock market investing. It is as if I am objecting at a wedding or laughing at a funeral.

"It's the thrill, the fantasy of it all," one coworker tells me, as she ponies up $20. "You'll be sorry if *we* win and *you* didn't put any money in," another woman snorts at me. Eyes roll when I mention that they could much likelier become millionaires by investing long term in the stock market. My admonitions are futile. I am a voice in the wilderness.

So I become the office troll for opposing the lottery pool. I am like Jonathan Swift advocating eating babies in a "modest proposal," although nobody sees any humor in my opposing the lottery. Although the odds are 10 million to one—and the money can be put to better use providing health insurance to the indigent—I am the evil guy of the moment for suggesting that there are guaranteed ways of making money that work for everyone.

It has always amazed me how many people have no idea, despite the tremendous wealth generated in the last fifteen years, that they too can benefit by investing and achieve reasonably high rates of success. They are put off by myths that only the financially savvy, the lucky, the highborn, or others get a piece of the pie—it will never be theirs to keep. Instead they play the lottery or go to casinos. It becomes a self-fulfilling prophecy: "I'll never be good with money, so I'll always have to work." For millions, this is their credo, and they *truly believe it*. I don't believe it, and I'll show you how a few simple principles will generate wealth over time no matter what you think about your lot in life. It all begins at your kitchen table.

Like John Muir's admonition, most of us are seeking a "fresh life." At some point in the future, we don't want to exist solely to pay bills. We want more from life and we want to be able to afford that life. We are striving for a New Prosperity, where our money is working for us to give us the life we *need* to live, instead of the other

KITCHEN-TABLE TIP

INVESTING VS. THE LOTTERY

This is an easy one, but ignored by millions. For the past thirty-seven years, even the worst stocks in the Dow Jones Industrial Average have returned about 16% a year. Investing a dollar a day instead of buying a one-dollar lottery ticket, you would have $1 million in your Dow "dogs" investment by age 57 (starting at age 16). By age 65, a dollar a day turns into $3.5 million.

SMALL SAVINGS YIELD BIG RESULTS

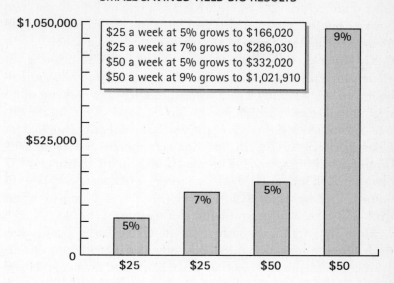

$25 a week at 5% grows to $166,020
$25 a week at 7% grows to $286,030
$50 a week at 5% grows to $332,020
$50 a week at 9% grows to $1,021,910

Source: Consumer Federation of America/Primerica.

way around. Surprisingly, the solution to our money woes lies within the bosom of our own families.

New Prosperity Starts in Your Family

I have to start this story by telling you about myself, my family, and my wife's family. None of us came into this world with anything except hope, our parents' love, and the promise of all creation. My wife, Kathleen, was born on the west side of Belfast, Northern Ireland, once known as "the ghetto of Europe." I met her and fell in love when she came to this country with her father and mother and two brothers. Her father worked in a low-paying job in a printing-ink plant. Kathleen worked as a restaurant hostess when she came here and later succeeded at computer graphics, sales, and her own business as a software consultant for Fortune 500 companies. Kathleen's brother Martin also worked in printing, later going into business with his mother in a custom window-treatment business. Steven, her other brother, has his own thriving business. They all survived poverty, bombs, tear gas, the British Army, the Irish Republican Army, and bad health to reap prosperity in the United States.

My father grew up with his mother and two sisters during the Depression. His mother raised him alone, as his father was an alcoholic and she was forced to divorce him after far too many of his steel mill paychecks were liquidated in the local saloon on the east side of Chicago Heights. Over the years, my father has applied his Depression-era survival instincts to save money and retire early from his teaching career. He invested heavily in his 403(b) and 457 plans through school, paid off the mortgage (six years early) on the home he purchased for $13,500 back in 1958, and did a lot of the work himself expanding our house during summer breaks.

More important, my father started saving early. His mother made him put his earnings in a post office savings account earning 1.5% per year (this was at a time when banks and savings and loans were failing). As a youth, he managed to put away $0.25 an hour (for 10-hour days) working on the onion farms of South Holland, Illinois, and the $1.10 a day he made caddying at a country club. He also learned how to play trumpet and played with big bands, saving that money in a Keogh retirement account. When he finished his master's degree at the University of Illinois-Champaign years later, not only was the degree paid for, he had $1,800 in savings.

When my three brothers and I were growing up, my father wasn't able to save much money for his own retirement, but ramped up his retirement plan contributions to $700 a month in the last twelve years of his high school teaching career. He also refrained from "moving up" to a bigger house. He consistently bought used cars and fixed them himself, bought used campers, and saved things that most people would have immediately dumped. He broke up an old piano and used it for any number of projects, including shelves. After twenty-five years, he still has pieces of it.

"I will continue to save those things that I deem to have some use or value," my father says defiantly, even though his family ribs him for failing to throw out junk. "I find that using up the things I've saved helps keep the creative bone alive and well in my head."

My mother also helped immensely by investing in her own individual retirement account, clipping coupons, shopping sales, and agreeing to go on our bargain camping vacations across the country. She was raised as an only child by her mother, as her father died at a young age. My parents saw each of their four boys go to college and bought their "honeymoon condo" in Florida. Of course, some of my parents' ability to save translated into wealth for my young family.

Despite no background in finance, Kathleen and I managed to save enough to remodel one house, keep two horses, and build a new home. In this book you'll learn more about us and our families and how we learned how to save and invest through investment clubs. We're the furthest thing from Ivy League, Wall Street types.

What we know is something millions have adopted, and our techniques are shared by those who have as little as $25 a month to invest. Do we practice some exotic stock market technique? Do we play the lottery and win? Hardly. We just fully fund our company retirement plans, stay invested, and reinvest our dividends. There isn't much more to it than that. And, despite everything that has happened to us, individually and collectively, our long-term investing will provide us with everything we'll need in a few years. We'd like to share these non-secrets with you. You needn't use us as an example—talk to anyone who lived through the Depression or World War II. They can provide hundreds of ways to save money that I only hint at in this book. The larger point is that savings—and your New Prosperity—begins within your family.

What This Book Will Do for You

I firmly believe that with some steady savings and investing you could well become a millionaire. Unlike the promises made by lotteries and game shows, however, it won't happen overnight and nobody will hand you a check. Making your money grow will be fun. You'll see results and you can measure them from year to year. Here's what I'll show you:

Find money to invest. It starts with pure savings. There are plenty of places to find money from the dollars you spend on your mortgage, your home, your transportation costs, and your credit. This book will contain at least 100 ways of saving money that you can employ.

Join the club. An investment club, that is. You can either join one, start one, or form a club of one (yourself). It's an exclusive club dedicated to learning how to invest. You'll enjoy it, and both your knowledge and money will grow.

Set up a parking place for your money. When you go to the supermarket or mall, you park your car and shop. When you save money, you park your money then invest. I'll show you the best places for your money while you are waiting or learning.

Fund your company plans. It doesn't matter if your company doesn't offer you a retirement plan. You can set up and fund your own rather easily.

Buy stocks for growth. I'll show you a really simple strategy that works over time. You can spend as little as $10 a month to start and put in place a program that will make your money grow for the rest of your life.

Buy mutual funds. If you don't want to buy individual stocks— or want to supplement your nest egg—I'll show you an incredibly easy strategy of picking four mutual funds for long-term growth.

Stay the course. I know the stock and bond markets make you nervous. They don't need to if you are a long-term investor and follow a few basic rules to stay the course.

Practice auto-pilot investing. I'll show you how to make saving and investing automatic and virtually invisible so that it lends balance to your life.

What I Won't Do

This is a short list, so I'll lay some notions to rest. I don't have an overnight plan to get rich quick. I won't insist that you stick to a budget (I don't know anyone who can). And I won't give you any theories on where the markets are going or stocks I think are sure winners. I will have plenty of suggestions of stocks and mutual funds to invest in, but I can't give you any surefire guarantees that they will blossom in a short period of time. My philosophy is based on investing over several decades' time. Time is on your side anyway, so why not take the slow, steady course to wealth?

What you will read in this book is a sampling of some strategies that have worked for millions of investors from all walks of life. You needn't have any special degrees, specialized knowledge, or incredible luck to make these ideas work for you. They work for any investor who is dedicated and consistent.

You'll read about investors from all walks of life who have succeeded or are on the path to success. I've deliberately avoided profiling millionaires or billionaires because they are not typical people. To give you some perspective, I've also interjected stories about myself, my family, and our family investment club. I haven't done this to boost my ego, but to show you our many failures and how we've overcome them to produce some solid savings and investment results. We aren't millionaires, but we are on the road to a New Prosperity.

Much of what I've discovered about saving and investing has come from interviewing hundreds of investors across the country, speaking at investment club fairs and researching investments over the past ten years. In this book, I make no assumptions as to where you are in life or how much money you have. You can use my strategies whether you are just starting out or have been struggling for years to put something away; there's no reason you can't make a fresh start. You can prosper if you apply yourself. There's no mystery about how money works and how it can become your servant instead of your master.

Your Goal: Finding a New Prosperity

New Prosperity is not a fixed, conventional idea of retirement. It represents a personal vision for your own life, a flexible arrangement where you can do what you need to do to balance your personal ecology; that is, form healthy relationships with the people and activities in your life that sustain you.

New Prosperity is having the time to spend with your children or grandchildren. Maybe it's working part-time and volunteering in the community. Maybe it's just adopting a four-day workweek. Or maybe it's pulling up stakes and buying that beach house. It's different for everyone, based on an idea that money works for us not to *buy* a lifestyle, but to make our lifestyles sustainable. Part and parcel of my personal ecology philosophy is that we look at how we spend our money and ask ourselves a direct question: Does what we buy add to our life or diminish it? If we are working overtime to pay for a car or mortgage, that's often not a sustainable activity. It throws our lives out of balance. We have less time for family and community, so others clearly suffer for the sake of paying a bill. It doesn't have to be that way if we learn what's essential and what's clearly not sustainable. Ecology stresses balance in the household, which is the meaning of ecology's Greek root *oikos*. We get our houses in order, so to speak.

In saving money, we are preserving our own natural resources, that is, our life energy. It comes back to us in so many ways, but we have to learn how to conserve this wonderful flux of power. It is what John Ruskin says in *Unto This Last,* "The rule and root of all economy—that what one person has, another cannot have; and that every atom of substance, of whatever kind, used or consumed, is so much human life spent."

In order to achieve a New Prosperity, our personal ecology needs to be in balance. Work, leisure, and family/community life become the three leaves of a flower that needs regular nourishment and pruning. We blossom when this happens. So why don't you decide what you would like to grow in your garden of New Prosperity. Do you want to retire at sixty? Buy that home in Florida? Start a business? Teach children in the inner city? Paint desert landscapes? Buy a motor home and see the continent? It's all possible in the personal utopia that comes with nurturing your New Prosperity. So write down your New Prosperity goals:

NEW PROSPERITY GOALS

1.
2.
3.
4.
5.

Once you've made your list, get a refrigerator magnet and stick your goals on the refrigerator. Look at them every day and ask yourself how you will achieve them. This book will provide guidance, but you will need to learn and actively shape your New Prosperity. Keep a journal of the things you are doing to achieve your goals. Write something down every month, week, or day, if you are so inclined. Every month go over your receipts (credit card, expenditures, checking account statements) and look at how you are spending money. What can you live without that can be saved toward your New Prosperity goals? Every dollar is a dollar closer to what you want.

To obtain this New Prosperity, you will need an ounce of courage and a pound of practice. It can be done if you ignore some of the superficial taunts and appeals of the advertising culture. As theologian Paul Tillich states, "It takes tremendous courage to resist the lure of appearances." You will gain courage, however, when you see how easy it is to achieve results.

Why Save?: A Reality Check

Nobody will argue when you say, "things have gotten so expensive, it's impossible to keep up." Homes, vehicles, college—even funerals—cost ten times more than they did in the late 1950s, when postwar prosperity seemingly blessed every home, households could be supported on one income. Cars, gas, food, and everything else were quite affordable on modest incomes.

Today, however, even though inflation has been held in check over the past fifteen years or so, every big-ticket item plunges us into a spiral of debt. And we work more to keep up with it. This is the dark side of the American economy going into the third millennium:

- **We're just not saving.** Despite the economic Mardi Gras of recent years, one-half of U.S. households have saved less than $1,000 in net financial assets and have "modest or no wealth," according to a survey commissioned by the Consumer Federation of America (CFA) and Primerica. Overall, the average U.S. savings rate (as a percentage of disposable income) is hovering around 2.4% annually, down from 8% about twelve years ago.
- **People work more, but net less savings.** Some 60% of U.S. households have two income earners today, versus less than 40% in 1950. But only 44% of households "with a currently employed householder will accumulate retirement savings that will be adequate to maintain the preretirement level of living through retirement years," according to a CFA/Ohio State study. All told, some 217 million Americans, or four out of five households, "are taking home a thinner slice of the economic pie than in 1977," according to a *New York Times* analysis of a Congressional Budget Office report.
- **We're living longer and we'll need more money.** The average life expectancy at birth today is 79.4 years for women and 73.9 years for men, according to the U.S. Administration on Aging. Half of all men who reach 65 can expect to live beyond age 80 and half of all women who reach 65 can expect to live past 84. "By the middle of the third millennium, a person who reaches age 65 might well be able to look forward to living another 35 or 40 more years," reports the National Summit on Retirement Savings. The average American will spend 18 years in retirement, notes the U.S. Department of Labor.
- **Social Security and pension plans alone won't be enough.** The maximum benefit (those workers earning at least $68,400) for Social Security will only replace less than one-quarter of retirement

income. Nearly 40% of the U.S. workforce has no company pension plan; only 19% of workers in small companies are offered one.

- **Even if company pension plans are offered, not all participate.** According to a Federal Reserve study, only 54% of U.S. households participate in company retirement plans. The lower the income, the lower the likelihood of participation. One-third of workers offered a defined-contribution—401(k)—plan don't even contribute, despite the record run-up in the stock market.

- **Low-income households, women, and minorities are hit the worst.** Some 70% of all elderly persons living below the poverty line are women, reports the Administration on Aging. One out of every six older women is a member of a minority group. Despite their tendency to live longer than men, women are less likely to have pension coverage due to their likelihood to be in and out of the workforce.

Numbers in Your Favor

The aforementioned statistics are scary, but you needn't judge yourself by them. To give you a glimpse of the silver lining, I'll quote one more figure from the 1999 Retirement Confidence Survey: "69 percent of [people calling themselves] savers said they could save an extra $20 a week for retirement . . . that equals $1,040 over the course of a year and more than $50,000 over 25 years at 5% return."

So forget these dire scenarios for now. What will reap a New Prosperity? A regular savings program that puts compound interest to work. To put this vehicle in gear, spend less than you earn, save for the short term, invest in stocks long-term and let it ride. This is the automatic route to wealth, and it's not complicated.

The Automatic Route to New Prosperity: How Compounding Works

If you can save at least 10% of your annual income—no matter how much you make—you will have your New Prosperity. Compound interest is the silent servant that will help get you there. Once you put the money aside, then the interest on your *principal*—your cash contribution—grows and builds more principal. If you've ever seen a bean sprout roots, it's the same principle. You start with one bean, which sprouts rootlets, which branch off into roots and a stem. The stem branches off to form leaves and in no time you're producing dozens of new beans. Money works the same way, starting with one dollar. Let's say you are saving $50 a month, which is only $12.50 a week or the cost of a few cups of coffee. It doesn't sound like much to start with, but let's see what happens.

THE MIRACLE OF COMPOUNDING

$12.50 per week = $50 per month = $600 per year
Invest that money at 8%/year = $29,451.02 after 20 years based on your total savings of only $12,000 and *$17,451.02* in compounded interest!

You put in $50 a month and end up with an *additional* $17,451.02. How does this happen? It's simply interest that compounds. The principal grows, then the interest is added over and over again. The bean sprouts roots, the stem shoots up, and the leaves grow out. One bean becomes many. That's all that's happening. Compound interest works for everyone. It requires no specialized knowledge other than the principal to start it running.

The above example is how compounding works on a basic level. Let's say you can save 10% of your annual household income. If you (and your significant other) net $40,000 and save $4,000 each year—or fund two Roth Individual Retirement Accounts (IRAs)—here's what happens:

THE MIRACLE OF SAVING 10% OF YOUR SALARY

$4,000 saved each year at 8% in a *tax-deferred* plan = *$146,891* after 20 years at 3% inflation rate. (Assuming a $40,000 household income.)

Source: Quicken.com.

This example is also a modest one. It assumes an 8% return, which is 3% a year less than the average return for stocks over the last seventy years. It also assumes that you're putting in only $4,000 and your employer isn't matching that amount. Employer matches or "found money"—that is a percentage of your pension contribution the employer contributes—are offered in most modern 401(k) plans or plans like SIMPLEs or Keoghs that you can set up yourself (see chapter 5). If saving 10% of your salary isn't possible, don't frown, just read the next chapter.

Where to Go from Here

You need to chart your course to New Prosperity, but you'll first need to see if you are saving enough money to get there. That's what the next chapter is all about. I'll show you dozens of ways to save money for investment. Once you have the money set aside, I'll show you where to put it and how you can make it grow even more.

SUMMARY

1. You'll do much better if you save on a regular basis instead of playing the lottery.
2. Your family is a great resource in finding ways to save.
3. Choose your own New Prosperity goals. Post them on your refrigerator and make regular updates on your progress.
4. Compound interest is a silent, consistent servant.
5. Put aside at least 10% of your annual net income and invest regularly.

CHAPTER 2

Found Money: How to Find
the Money to Invest

Let the man of means spend according to his means: and the man whose resources are restricted, let him spend according to what Allah has given him. Allah puts no burden on any person beyond what he has given him. After a difficulty, Allah will soon grant relief.

—The Holy Qur'an

Robin and Danny Gagliardi are living the New Prosperity lifestyle without suffering the travails of suffocating bills. They are doing it on just over $17,000 a year. Are they on welfare? Did they inherit money? Hardly. They made a few key decisions early and are reaping the benefits as Danny works on his Ph.D. in mathematics at North Carolina State University and Robin stays home with their sons Zachary, Michael, and Eric.

The former New Yorkers had the life that is supposed to be the envy of most Americans, but now it's even better—even though they are earning much less. Danny, forty, worked as a programmer for IBM for nine years. Robin, thirty-five, was an investment banker. They lived modestly in New York City on the Upper West Side, making $100,000 together, and saving one salary. In North Carolina now, they own their beautiful home outright in an upscale neighborhood of professionals.

While renting an apartment in New York, Robin and Danny bought a house in upstate Ossining and fixed it up to rent it out, later selling it and using the proceeds to buy a house for cash. They took out a fifteen-year mortgage on the house, prepaid the mortgage so that it was paid off in four years, and did all of the fix-up work themselves. They bought used cars, saw cheap matinees, and cooked a lot of meals themselves. When they were ready for their New Prosperity move and Danny decided to work on his Ph.D., they targeted a relatively inexpensive part of the country (relative to New York) and vowed to live on Danny's stipend as a research assistant while he finished his degree.

"We're advocates on waiting to buy what you really want," Robin says of their comfortable lifestyle. "We have no monthly budget, but we either look at what we want and wait, or we don't buy it. We've never had a car loan and always buy used cars."

Like many of their friends, Robin and Danny could have lived in pricier digs in suburban New York. But Robin admits that though they would have been living in better surroundings, they would not have been living *well*. Not that they are always shopping at tag sales or clipping coupons, which Robin isn't crazy about. They do the things they want to do and picked a place where they could walk almost anywhere.

"We don't feel deprived. We live in a $250,000 home now. I will never have to work full-time the rest of my life and we are doing things slowly. We're saving for a bigger car and our three kids' college educations." They invest in mutual funds for this purpose and have purchased individual stocks such as Xerox and AT&T.

There is something simple yet elegant in how Robin and Danny live. They haven't chosen to live like hermits, but they've chosen to live simply and eliminate most people's two biggest debts—a mortgage and a car loan. Robin rues the fact that one of her friends in New York takes her children to the country club for lunch every day and sighs that far too many people like her friend earn hundreds of thousands of dollars yet are struggling to make ends meet.

The satisfaction in having a financial life well under control is evident in the serene tone in Robin's voice. "Everybody has to be

"GOOD DEBT" COSTS LESS

Loan rates

The average interest rate on a 30-year home mortgage is 8.1%.* How that compares with other types of loans:

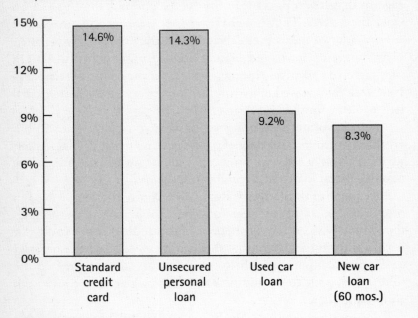

At time of publication.

able to sleep at night. I don't want to go back to work to pay bills. We live on a block with doctors and bankers—all in much worse financial shape than we are. We are living a better life with less."

The keys to Robin and Danny's success boil down to few essentials of money management. They save more than they spend. They don't get sucked into the vacuum of "better life through spending" advertising. Here are some other things they've done:

- They've realized that new cars depreciate the second you drive them off the lot. They save up and buy used for less (they are getting ready to buy new when they've saved enough cash).

- They fully invest in Individual Retirement Accounts.
- They use money market accounts as holding places for their money.
- For long-term investing, they invest in growth and small-company growth stock funds.
- They buy food in bulk to save and cook meals at home. Danny buys fifty pounds of pasta at a time.
- They decide what they want and need and purchase accordingly. They wait to buy the big items until they have the money.
- They look at what they've spent every month and save what's left over.

"Pocket change can add up." Robin should know. Her father, Marc Eisenson, edits *The Pocket Change Investor* newsletter with Nancy Castleman. There's nothing Marc and Nancy don't know about saving.

- They pay off their mortgages early by adding money to principal every month.
- They know that saving buys them security and freedom.

Robin and Danny Gagliardi are realistic role models. They have done well in the prime of their lives because they save and ignore nearly all of the sales pitches being hurled at them. For most Americans, though, the inability to save is a mystery and the culprits aren't always obvious.

It's Hard to Save: Some Insights

I was on a plane to Pittsburgh (more on what I was doing in Pittsburgh in chapter 3), when I noticed a flashing message on the seat in front of me. Actually, it was a flashing message on the *phone* on the seat in front of me. The LED sign on the top of the handset was imploring me to send e-mail and data on this particular phone, even though I was some 30,000 feet in the air and clutching said seat as the intrepid pilot was navigating a thunderstorm. It suddenly occurred to me that there are ever new ways to make us consume more of whatever product or service, no matter where we are.

There were little cartoon characters on my daughter's diapers, which were, of course, designed to get me to buy more of a certain brand of diapers. You can't walk into any discount store and buy a pair of kids' shoes or certain articles of clothing (sleepwear in particular) without a licensed character from Disney movies, cable, or public television appearing on it. These overpriced products (you pay for Disney's advertising on them) are largely aimed at parents, but increasingly target toddlers to identify the characters and force the buying decision. You ever try to argue with a screaming two-year-old dead-set on Barney in a crowded store? Even in the hospital—and in the ob-gyn's office—you are presented with branded "samples" of everything from baby powder to formula. The pleasant receptionists in the baby doctor's office even encourage you to "sign up for more" samples, a ploy designed to get you onto endless mailing lists for more and more baby stuff, magazines, and health care products. I'm working backward on the great chain of consumerism, which starts before birth. When does it stop? How can we avoid it and not spend money on things we may not need?

The Torrent of Advertising

To say that the torrent of marketing to every human being at every age in Western culture is relentless is an understatement. The Internet—our newest and most powerful information medium—is awash in advertising. You already know that advertising drives newspapers, magazines, radio, and television—even public radio and television accepts sly "sponsorships" that promote corporate images. Even when we leave urban areas to get away from billboards, computers, and broadcast media, the "buy message" follows us. I recently went bird-watching in the Liberty Prairie Preserve near my home and was greeted by a discarded styrofoam McDonald's coffee cup. The golden arches are everywhere. My daughter identified them with McDonald's before she was two years old, even though she had scarcely seen more than a few hours of broadcast television at that point.

Despite twenty-four-hour advertising, most of us don't buy everything we see. Danny and Robin Gagliardi certainly don't. The psychology of "24-7" advertising, however, is more subtle and often debilitating. As "consumers," we lose the focus of what's important in our lives. We are turned into "units" who function based on having and buying things versus balancing our needs. These are two different concepts that most producers of consumer goods and services would like you not to examine carefully. It's somewhat subversive to say that you don't need most of what's advertised. Do you need to know about several hundred thousand brands of beer, personal care products, or toothpaste? Will one brand of hand lotion make a difference in your life? Can you justify spending $50,000 on a car versus $20,000? Will one brand of shampoo give you eternal youth?

Branded into Oblivion

The "branding" of America is the most insidious part of our culture. Now entire personalities are subsumed into brands. Michael Jordan is a brand. Martha Stewart is a brand. Every supermodel and pop singer is a brand. There are few places you can escape logos such as the Nike "swoosh" or Mickey Mouse ears. The brands scream only two messages at us: "You're not good enough," and "Spend."

I know it's un-American to question the foundation of advertising. These myriad lies help industries employ people, who can maintain their livelihoods, get the global economy humming, and pay taxes to support essential services such as schools, firehouses, and police forces. What I question with vigor, however, is the dangerous imbalance consumer spending creates—an imbalance that disturbs your "personal ecology"—your relationship with self, health, family, community, and true wealth.

How Advertising Distorts the Need for Saving

Advertising is a huge reason why people don't invest. Advertising is a shell game that sets us up for the quick thrill, eternal youth in a bottle, sex at the beach by drinking a brand of beer and buying a lot of things that do absolutely nothing for us. Instead of saving the money we would be spending on some gadget, vehicle, or wardrobe, we could be investing in our children and ourselves. Advertising is the deep end of the ocean. When we succumb and sink into it, there's no bottom to the spending.

The great bathysphere of advertising is television, one of the greatest selling mediums of all time. The more TV we take in, the more advertising we absorb. The medium is the message, after all. I know this is sounding like a sermon, and I hate preaching, but let's look at the research and how spending and (not) saving are related when it comes to TV and advertising:

- The more TV a person watches, the more he/she spends (based on the advertising they absorb). It's like exposure to lead. The more it gets into your system, the more your faculties of reasoning are impaired. Dr. Juliet Schor, a Harvard researcher and author of *The Overspent American* (Basic Books, 1998), found in a study conducted of TV watchers, that for every extra hour spent (above an average) watching TV, the subjects spent an additional $208 per week. On average they spent an additional $2,300 a year in unplanned expenditures.

- TV and advertising distorts the view we have of ourselves. Advertising is designed to make you feel uncomfortable about yourself, your possessions, and everything around you. If you are perfectly secure and comfortable, then you won't feel a need to buy the thousands of products being marketed. Dr. Schor found that though 70% in her survey described average Americans as materialistic, only 8% said they were materialistic *themselves.*

- Too much TV watching costs society dearly. There are more than 2,000 studies linking excessive TV watching to violence, obesity, attention deficits, lower academic achievement, and reduced family time, according to the U.S. Surgeon General. Some two million TV commercials will be seen by the average American by the time they reach 65; 360,000 before children graduate from high school. Americans spend something like 40% of their free time in front of the tube. That's more than 11.8 hours a day for most Americans. When do we have time to work, save, or be with our families?

Turn Off the Tube and Start Saving

You know where this train is going. Let's stop at the station first for our first savings strategy: *Turn off the TV.* Just try it for a day, a week, a month, a year. My family did. I'll be honest with you that we didn't stop spending money on things we didn't need, but we were able to nearly fully fund our retirement plans, our daughter's education fund, and spend as much time as we liked being with *ourselves.* We discovered we didn't miss the shows our friends were watching, we had plenty of time for whatever we wanted to do, we didn't obsess about our general appearances or get into debt by buying ever-larger cars, audiovisual equipment, or any number of other things. Moreover, we found that we could entertain ourselves quite well, read lots of books, rented videos once a week, and our toddler daughter acquired language skills at a pace above and beyond her contemporaries.

"Consumption ties a tighter knot between work and free time than any of the schemes of reformers, employers, or governments," notes Joanne Ciulla in *The Working Life: The Modern Betrayal of Modern Work* (Times Books, 2000). "The market tempts people with more leisure opportunities than they can afford or have time to enjoy."

The Real Truth about Saving and Spending

Consumerism is not the enemy, but like most things done in excess, it can become destructive or we become willing slaves to it. It also compels us to work more than we'd like and be apart from our families.

If you take away nothing else from this treatise on cutting out the influence advertising has on your life, know this: If you spend less, you'll quickly save more. I know this sounds like a big "duh," but here's how it works: Money needlessly squandered can double, even triple, if put into modest savings/investment plans. For this process to work, however, you have to save.

There is a powerful spiritual component to savings as well. Being in deep debt is a form of slavery—to your creditors. If you are working just to pay bills, you are shackled to what you owe. It's a lonely, impoverishing situation. Mother Teresa noticed it when she visited the United States:

> There are many kinds of poverty. Even in countries where the economic situation seems to be a good one, there are expressions of poverty hidden in a deep place, such as the tremendous loneliness of people who have been abandoned and who are suffering.

You doubtless have heard economists bemoaning Americans' poor savings rate relative other industrialized countries. Of course, you could argue that a U.S. savings rate of 2.3% (down from 8.3% in 1991) is *good* for the consumer economy. As *Washington Post* columnist Robert Samuelson observes, "Every percentage point drop in the savings rate is worth about $66 billion in consumer spending." While that's certainly good for merchants' cash registers short term, it's robbing individuals of the prosperity they'll need in twenty or thirty years. That leads me to a fairly ironclad savings strategy: *If you do nothing else, trim your spending and save what you would have spent in a tax-deferred account.*

The math of this strategy is rather elegant and foolproof. Say you have a nominal pretax household income of $50,000 (you probably make more money on the side, but let's not talk about that for now). You're in the 28% federal tax bracket, 5% state income tax, and your money is growing at 10% a year pretax, which is roughly what the stock market has been averaging over the last 65 years. How much will you have in 20 years?

Initial investment: $5,000 or $416.66 a month for every year
Inflation rate of 3% per year
Total after 20 years @ 10% per year = <u>$169,920</u> in taxable account
Total in a tax-deferred account (company plan, IRA, etc.) = <u>$219,096</u>

Okay, what about making money on the side? Maybe you take a second job or start a little business or your spouse brings in some money. Add $25,000 to your household income and you're taking in $75,000, of which you save $7,500 each year. Using the same tax rates @ 10% per year, the picture brightens considerably:

Total after 20 years ($7,500/year or $625 a month) = $\underline{\$419,342}$ in a
    taxable account
Total in a tax-deferred account = $\underline{\$580,071}$

Now here's where we have some fun. To quote Mick Jagger and Keith Richard, "Tiiiiime is on my side, yes it is!" Add another ten years to the time you are saving that $625 a month and you're doing much better than most television game show contestants. Now the numbers look really swell and your New Prosperity is obtainable within your working life:

Total after 30 years @ 10% = $\underline{\$746,951}$ in a taxable account
Total in a tax-deferred account = $\underline{\$1,222,161}$

Do you want to become a millionaire? You *can* do this without winning the lottery, without taking extraordinary risks, without selling your belongings or even earning a big salary. What's $625 a month? A car payment and a health club membership? Eating in a few nights a week? Going without cable TV and a boat? This is not a matter of deprivation, it's a guaranteed New Prosperity, because the miracle of compounding demands so little of your time, so little actual thinking that it's like the sun coming up every day. What's the catch? *Saving at least 10% of your annual income regularly and . . . Fully Funding Your Tax-Deferred Vehicles.*

Here's the plan: In subsequent chapters, I'll tell you how you can easily achieve that modest 10% return—and then some—and how to set up your tax-deferred vehicles through your employer or by yourself. But before we explore those wonderful details, let's see how you can pony up $500 to $750 a month for your New Prosperity plan. I'll even do the math for you. All you have to do is turn off the TV and start saving.

Triple S: Simple Super Savings

I don't claim miracles, but you can employ my "Triple S" strategy no matter how little (or how much) education you have. It utilizes the miracle of compound interest and a little discipline—you have to save the money. The compounding works automatically; the discipline is up to you. It's easy to save on hundreds of relatively minor items—and I'll provide a list of them at the end of the chapter. To find some big money for investing, though, you need to concentrate on three areas in your life: housing, vehicles, and debt. These three are not only the three biggest areas where we spend money (college, weddings, and funerals are further down the list), but you can save money on any or all of these areas. Since housing is where the heart is, let's start there.

Housing: The Truth about What You Need to Do

A great deal of the conventional wisdom about housing is misleading. True, buying a house is one of the most costly financial transactions you'll make (probably two or three times in your life), but home-buying has always been regarded the wrong way by most Americans. For generations, owning a home outright has been the source of quintessential American pride. Once people got past a certain age, they couldn't wait to pay off the mortgage. Today, however, with corporate relocations, mergers, downsizings, and the dot.com economy moving people where the growth is, a home is no longer the solid investment it was. In fact, for many in our highly mobile economy, the home is not an investment at all.

My parents bought a home as soon as they could move out of an apartment in 1956. With four boys, a place in the south suburbs of Chicago was all they needed. It was a Cape Cod with only one bathroom, a basement, and an attic that they later converted to a bedroom for my brother Steve and me. My dad later built on a bedroom, half-bath, and a family room on his summer vacation. Soon after we all left home for either college or jobs, my parents paid off the mortgage. A few years after that, they bought a condo in

Florida, where they spend the winters. For millions of World War II generation couples, paying off the mortgage, or "burning the note," was the ultimate expression of freedom. Bolstered by Medicare, Social Security, and defined-benefit pensions, they waltzed into retirement wealthy and debt-free and were able to travel and enjoy their golden years.

In today's economic environment, however, there are new ways to regard a mortgage debt. The most fundamental way of looking at a mortgage is to regard it as a debt security, which is a promise to pay a party over time for the use of their money. Since mortgage defaults are rare—and you can sell the home if you get in too deep—a mortgage note is practically guaranteed money for investors. Even if you are the mortgagee (you're paying off the debt), you can see the note like a bond. Although you're not getting interest payments, you can deduct the finance charges, property taxes, and "points" on the loan. Though you're not getting paid directly, the "return" on this note to you is essentially the rate of inflation plus any real estate market appreciation.

Why does a mortgage pay *you* a return? Because the underlying property is appreciating with inflation. Real estate values increase over time because property becomes an increasingly scarce commodity in urban areas. Sure, new homes are built all the time. But a home is a fixed asset in a fixed location. People rarely move their homes and the intrinsic value of the property goes up as more homes are built and property becomes more scarce. You also reap a premium if your local economy grows and the existing housing stock shrinks. Then people are willing to pay more for an increasingly dear asset. It's the law of supply and demand. When a local economy turns down the opposite is true. Fewer homeowners are able to live in the community and more homes are for sale than sold. This happens in any factory or mill town when the main employer shutters the gates, or when regional industries falter as they did in the industrial heartland in the early '80s or in Southern California (aerospace contractors) in the early '90s.

As a debt security, your mortgage has economic value. It allows you to retain and grow equity. Remember, the single most valuable part of the mortgage is to build principal. That's money you keep, although it's *illiquid*. You can only get at it through a home equity loan, refinancing, or selling your house. It's what you do with principal that determines how much wealth your home will generate. Interest and escrow—the two other components—don't make any money for you, although I'll show you how to lower those costs as well.

Saving by Paying Down Mortgage Principal

Over any period of time, the lender makes most of its money from the interest. That's why lenders only provide "Rule of 72" bank mortgages, which load most of the interest in the first third of the loan term. They want their money up front and you don't start really paying down principal until they've soaked you for thousands in interest payments. The best way, however, of reducing your mortgage debt—and build wealth—is to pay down principal, not interest.

Paying down principal reduces the term of the loan, thereby reducing the total interest. What most homeowners don't know is that they can pay down as much principal as they like every month. You could pay off a 30-year note in ten years if you paid down enough principal. Unless a bank imposes a "prepayment penalty," which is illegal in most states, paying down principal gives you more freedom. Without a mortgage payment down the road, you are free to save and invest your former mortgage payment. Then you only have to worry about taxes. That's what my parents did, but it only makes sense if you plan to stay in one home until you pay off the note. Those who are highly mobile or need to relocate won't benefit from this strategy too much, although the principal is almost always yours to keep. I say "almost" because depressed local real estate markets will reduce the value of your home.

I first learned about the mortgage prepayment strategy through Marc Eisenson, who wrote *The Banker's Secret* book and software. Here's how paying down principal works:

MORTGAGE STRATEGY #1: PAY IT OFF

Pay down your principal by adding to the principal payment every month. This strategy is best for:

- Those who have fully funded/tax-deferred retirement/company plans.
- Those with extra money to invest.
- Those who don't plan to move within the next 15 years or more.

Here's how it works:

$151,000 mortgage @ 7.8% annual percentage rate ($150,000 plus some financed closing fees) = $240,316 total principal and interest over 30 years *if you make all 360 payments*

- Add $50 a month to principal = pay off in 25 years, four months, saving $42,182.55 in interest
- Add $75 to principal each month = pay off in 24 years, saving $57,341.65 in interest
- Add $100 a month = pay off in 23 years, saving $70,020
- Add $125 = pay off in 21 years, 7 months, saving $80,890.29
- Add $150 = pay off in 20 years, 9 months, saving $90,186.46

Source: The Banker's Secret, Good Advice Press, Box 78, Elizaville, NY 12523.

The idea here is straightforward: The more you pay off principal each month, the shorter the loan term and the more interest you save. Of course, this requires a real commitment to your home and community—assuming you won't move and have the extra money to invest. It works and it's liberating because one day you won't have the biggest expense of your life staring you in the face. You won't have to work as much or as hard. Robin and Danny did it. All it takes is the will to want that New Prosperity sooner rather than later.

When You *Don't* Want to Pay Off the Mortgage

The obverse side of the principal pay-down strategy for short-term homeowners is to find the lowest-cost, shortest-term, lowest-rate mortgage you can find. Better yet, rent an apartment and you don't have to deal with thousands of dollars in closing costs, lawyer's fees, taxes, and maintenance. If you have no interest in building equity over time, then renting is probably a good idea. Some people just don't want the trouble of owning a house. After a period of time, you have to paint, replace the roof, furnace, air conditioning, and fix an endless number of things. You never build equity by paying for repairs (roofing, paint, etc.). Remodeling is another suspect way of building equity.

Our first home after we sold our "honeymoon condo" was a single-family ranch with 2.5 acres in Wauconda, Illinois, which is about 50 miles northwest of Chicago. At the time, we were making a good income between us, so Kathleen indulged in her hobby by buying a horse. Unbeknownst to us, the horse she bought was pregnant and delivered a foal as a complete surprise to us one spring evening. We kept the foal despite my best instincts and bought the ranch house, which came with a dilapidated barn. The seller's prayers were answered when they saw us coming.

The house itself should have been a candidate for a big explosive charge. A bulldozer would have improved the secluded, wooded lot immensely. Being the naive, ex-urban pioneers we were, we decided to fix up the house and barn, improve the property, and keep the horses. We soldiered on, repairing a house that needed a new roof, walls, windows, heating, air conditioning, a driveway, plumbing, electrical, and insulation. Yes, we bought a house that needed *everything redone.* We kept one picture window and the fireplace. The house was structurally unsound and the wind blew through in certain places. The barn was sinking. During heavy rains, the low front yard turned into a lake. We also converted the one-car garage into an office and bedroom and the central full bath into a powder room.

When we finished our *nine-year* remodeling journey, we welcomed our daughter Sarah Virginia into the world and the horses then became a dangerous and neglected hobby for Kathleen. It took us another year to decide that updating the house even more meant pricing ourselves out of the neighborhood, of mostly retirees.

After spending $70,000 on repairs and updating every room, we decided to take our equity elsewhere. We built a new, energy-efficient, low-maintenance home in a neighborhood with young families, trails, a beach, and plenty of community activities. Although the new house was one-third larger, had a two-car garage, two-and-half baths, and a huge basement, it cost twice what we paid for the old house. Our mortgage payment, however, was about the same, since every penny we netted from the old house went into equity for the new home (taxes, however would be much higher).

Our decision shows the alternative of what you *don't* need to do with your home equity; that is, spend it. Far too many people have "tapped" home equity in refinancing or borrowed against it for cars, boats, and vacations. We certainly were tempted to take that equity and invest it in the stock market, where we could have reaped a much higher return. We also could have spent it to buy a car, furniture, and lots of other things. To us, though, the relatively low-returning equity was security for the future in the context of a modest mortgage payment. We also are working to pay down the principal and pay off the loan before our children are in college.

A mortgage, you will recall, is essentially a bond that will pay you a nominal rate of return based on the rate of inflation plus any local premium. When inflation rises, the underlying value of this bond—in your real estate—also rises. But when inflation is low (under 5%) and stocks are in favor, your money can garner a better return in stocks. So it's little surprise that during the heyday of the bull market, home equity has shrunk relative to financial assets.

In 1998, the primary residence accounted for only 28 percent of average household assets in a Federal Reserve Board survey, down from nearly one-third in 1989. That's because home prices were outpaced by soaring stock prices. The median home price was $100,000 in 1998, up from only $95,600 in 1995. In the same period, the average value of household financial assets rose 36%. So, assuming you invested that $95,600 at 12% a year (36% divided by three) in a tax-deferred account, you'd have $122,914 in only three years. Which is the better investment, your home or a stock fund? You could boost your pretax return by basically investing in an average-performing mutual fund. So, the second alternative strategy is *keep* your mortgage and invest in stocks. Here's how it works:

MORTGAGE STRATEGY #2: INVEST IN STOCKS

In a low-inflation environment, invest in low-cost stocks/mutual funds that grow at double-digit returns and reinvest the dividends. Keep paying down your mortgage as much as you can. Set a target date for when you want to pay off your mortgage and boost your principal payments accordingly. Use this strategy if:

- Your company plans are *not* fully funded.
- You may move within 5–10 years.
- You just don't have the money to invest in principal.

This second mortgage strategy gives you an end-date for your mortgage and helps you build your New Prosperity fund through stocks. This strategy works best if you haven't fully funded your retirement plans and fund your principal prepayments with whatever is left over.

As if two strategies weren't enough, here's a third: Sell your house and *invest* the equity. Under the new tax laws, any gain from a home sale up to $500,000 (for married couples filing jointly) is yours tax free. Here are a few ways to work this strategy:

MORTGAGE STRATEGY #3: INVEST THE EQUITY

This strategy works best if you have a lot of flexibility. Generally, empty-nesters can employ this if they don't want or need a larger house anymore. It will work if:

- You sell your home to downsize to a smaller home or condo. Take the remaining equity and invest it in stocks or stock mutual funds. This strategy is best for those who are underfunded in their tax-deferred plans and who just haven't saved much of anything while the kids were at home.

▪ Sell your home and buy a less expensive house (with lower taxes and maintenance) and use the equity to eliminate your mortgage. Except for taxes, a huge share of your take-home pay can now be invested for your New Prosperity. This strategy also works if you simply have too much home for your budget or one spouse either loses a job or quits work.

Pick the Mortgage Strategy That's Right for You

As you can see, there's no one right way to do your mortgage. As a debt, it's "good debt" as long as you are getting a return on it and you can afford to carry it. If you are barely making your mortgage and tax payments now, strategy #3 is certainly the most viable, provided you can find decent housing at a lower price in the neighborhood you want. All three strategies are designed to produce significant savings either short- or long-term, depending on when you need the money. As with all other savings, the longer you have to compound the principal (mortgage strategy #3), the better, so once again, time is on your side no matter which strategy you choose.

Affordable Wheels

Americans love their cars the way dogs love walks, bones, and petting. We talk about vehicles, cast them in movies, make romance in them, and go to work in them. Some of us are even born in them. They drive our imaginations like no other cultural icon.

Unfortunately, the American obsession with vehicles is getting a bit out of control. We tend to spend too much on them and forget that they are machines and lose value over time. There's only a handful of (vintage) vehicles that are truly considered investments, and most of us can't afford them in the first place. So I hate to be un-American, but four wheels should not double your household debt load. There's nothing wrong with getting in debt over a vehicle, as long as that debt is short-lived, but that's not the case with families that can't seem to save money.

It won't surprise you to hear that many households are paying more for transportation than property taxes and interest on their mortgage. I know, with a three-year lease, you get a new car that's always under warranty. But what are you getting for it? Does a new car add to your prosperity or steal from it? Is the new-car smell worth spoiling your future security?

How much can you save by deferring a big vehicle purchase or not leasing? I don't recommend leasing unless you can write off the lease payments for business purposes. Let's start with a $300-a-month loan or lease payment. I'm assuming that you're either waiting to buy a new vehicle or paying off an existing vehicle with the intention of saving the former payment. For this example, I'm going real conservative and assuming you can invest the difference in a short-term bond or money market fund. So, let's see what your $300 ($3,600 a year) looks like over 10 years:

SAVING THE CAR PAYMENT

$300 a month @ 6% a year over 10 years = $48,979
In a tax-deferred account at age 65 = $203,874 (assuming you start saving at age 40).

So what's my point? How can you possibly *live* without a vehicle or a constant car payment? How do you get around without wheels? Here are a few transportation strategies:

- Live with one vehicle. If one spouse can take the train to work, the other can drive.
- Don't buy new. As soon as you drive off the lot, your vehicle is worth 20% to 30% less, yet you're still paying interest and principal on the full purchase price. Hardly seems fair, does it?
- Buy "program" cars, second- or third-year cars with warranties or vehicles coming off leases. You'll save several thousand dollars and be able to pay them off in shorter periods of time or with cash, if you have it.

KITCHEN-TABLE TIP

The average U.S. family spends more on transportation than on food, health care, or taxes—one-sixth of the household budget. Although the ideal car is fully paid for and low maintenance, here's a good profile of inexpensive wheels. Older, smaller cars cost less to run and insure. After a while, check on the car's book value, then drop your collision and comprehensive insurance coverage—if you can afford it. If you've saved, you can cover the car if something happens to it, but this strategy also works if you keep the car more than five years. In a new car, look for a fuel-efficient car and maintain it well with regular oil changes, tune-ups, tire inflation/rotation, and maintenance. You'll save thousands of dollars that you can instead invest in your New Prosperity fund.

- Use an auto broker. That includes the dozens of Internet brokers listed in the Resources section at the end of the book. Find the lowest price. Negotiate for it. Forget dealers that offer you one price. If they don't deal, you don't deal.

- Get as close to the invoice price as possible. Get the prices from *Consumers Digest* magazine or www.consumersdigest.com. Shop near the end of a model year on the last day of a month on a Saturday. Dealers will want to move cars to refresh their inventory and "make their numbers" for the month and year. We did this and got a great deal and were prepared to walk away unless we got our price.

- Get the shortest loan term possible in simple interest. Finance companies and banks will try to get you into a "Rule of 72" loan that front-loads interest payments into the early years of the loan. Get a loan where each interest payment is the same every month and pay it off early. Forget about five-year loans.

- Don't lease unless you can write off the lease payments for business. The pro-leasing argument goes "lease payments make the vehicle much more affordable, so we can buy a more expensive vehicle." At the end of the lease, chances are you'll want another new car and you'll have no equity and sign up for another lease. Where's the savings?

• Buy a used car through a third party, not a dealer. That way you can avoid the $1,000 to $2,000 markup per vehicle. Do your research on reliability through *Consumer Reports.* Buy the least expensive, most reliable used car you can. Keep it maintained on a regular basis. Vehicles never really "pay for themselves," but you certainly can lower your ownership costs by following the owner's manual and replacing parts when needed. If you buy a car through a classified ad, ask to see repair receipts.

• Don't use a home equity loan to buy a vehicle unless you have no other choice. This is a "robbing Peter to pay Paul" sort of proposition. You are financing a depreciating asset with an appreciating one (your home). So what if the interest is deductible and you're getting a better interest rate? You still have to pay back the loan. If, God forbid, you default on the home equity loan, the bank can foreclose on your home—all for a set of wheels. You also have to repay the loan when you sell your home.

• If you want a larger vehicle, buy the one with the most interior space, not the most exterior glitz. This is one of many arguments against sport-utility vehicles, which are overpriced trucks. If interior space is what you need for passengers, kids, pets, and cargo, then go with a minivan or station wagon. You'll not only get more flexibility (seats fold down, pop out, etc.), but your gas mileage will be better, your insurance will be lower, and you won't be ripped off.

AN ARGUMENT AGAINST REALLY BIG VEHICLES

1. Bigger Vehicles Cost a Lot More to Operate when the Price of Gas Rises
   • Fill-up (10.3 gallons) for a Geo Metro @ $2/gallon = $522/year additionally (vs. $.99/gallon)
   • Fill-up (44 gallons) for Ford Excursion @ $2/gallon = $2,293/year additionally (vs. $.99 a gallon)
2. How much would you make if you invested the difference in gas expenses alone for the two vehicles?

$1,000 invested in Motorola stock (1999) @ $65/share = $2,707 one year later, for a gain of 17%. Of course, this is an exceptional example; the main point is that you can do much better if you spend less on vehicles and invest the difference in savings.

- Don't get financing through the dealer. Shop around at local banks and credit unions. Never sign up for "credit life" insurance that will pay off the loan if you can't make payments or die. The vehicle can be sold if something happens. This is the most expensive and worthless (to you) insurance in the world.
- Approach your relatives and friends first. Maybe they'll swap a vehicle or sell you one at a discount. Ask them about their experience with the vehicle. If they've maintained it well, that's a better selling point than a warranty on a used-car lot.
- Don't buy extended warranties. Buy reliable vehicles instead. I never trusted manufacturers who sold them.
- Shop for options that add value to the vehicle. Trim, moonroofs, fender skirts, and purely cosmetic additions aren't what you need. Geographic positioning systems and neat sound systems are gee-whiz items but not worth the additional cost.

Credit Cards: All You Need to Know

For years, I was convinced I needed several credit cards to charge different types of purchases. I used department store cards in department stores. For travel items, I used American Express. I obtained a low-interest card for long-term purchases. And I had a card that accrued frequent-flyer miles for short-term purchases. My wallet was as fat as a bagel, but I was doing exactly what credit card marketers wanted me to do, and it was only throwing money into their coffers and putting me deeper into debt.

Millions of Americans have fallen into the marketing abyss that credit card companies have created. As a result, they've been submerged in debt that they can easily avoid. The Federal Reserve Board has found that the amount owed by the average American household ballooned some 42% from $23,400 to $33,300 between 1995 and 1998. All told, some 74% of American households are in debt and hold an average $1,700 credit card balance. For households that have fully funded retirement plans and enough short-term savings, this short-term debt is usually not a problem. It gets to be a debilitating financial condition, however, when you are paying more to the credit card company than to your own New Prosperity fund.

There's nothing wrong with having one credit card. That's all you need, and make it pay you. Want to save for a car? Get an auto card. Want frequent-flyer miles? Get an airline card. *One* card from one of the major issuers (VISA or Mastercard) is generally accepted worldwide. Don't waste your time with department store, catalog, or other kinds of cards. You don't need them, the finance charges are higher, and you'll feel obligated to shop more.

The most traditional argument for having a credit card is that you "need it for emergencies." If you are adequately funding your short-term savings (see next chapter), then this argument is a fallacy. You need a credit card to rent a car and some other things. But aside from that, you can live without one. Maybe you *can't* live without a credit card and you have a significant balance staring at you every month. How do you know if you're in deep water?

How much credit card debt is too much? If you can't pay your other bills or "pay yourself first" for your own future. It's that simple. You don't even need to do the math. Just pay off your credit card each month and avoid installment loans. Pay cash whenever possible. If you don't have the money (except for a vehicle or home), don't buy it. Naturally, you'll encounter emergencies when the water heater breaks, you have engine problems, or some unexpected expenses pop up. For those unintended consequences of life, you can fall back on your short-term savings (yet another reason to read the next chapter). If you have a credit card balance or installment loan, here's how much you can save by diverting your debt payments into New Prosperity savings:

HOW MUCH CAN YOU SAVE BY PAYING OFF CREDIT CARDS?

Let's say your credit card payments are about $200 a month or $2,400 a year. What happens if those debt payments are saved at a 6% return = $29,013 (after taxes) in 10 years?

For the big payoff, put $200 a month into a tax-deferred account at 6% (you can do much better than this) and if you start at 40 you'll have $135,916 by age 65.

What is the best way of dealing with credit? Aside from deciding upon the mortgage strategy that is right for you, use credit as little as possible. Yes, stay out of short-term debt if you can. Unlike the mortgage and vehicle strategies, it doesn't get more complicated than that. I hate to disappoint you, but the best short-term debt is no debt.

A few guidelines will keep you out of trouble with credit:

1. Pay off your short-term debts every month. Once you fall behind on the "minimum" payments, you are only paying off interest and not the principal. The interest compounds every month, but not for you—for the bank.

2. Use credit for emergencies, but only for the "grace period" of the credit card. Avoid finance charges by paying off your bill within the grace period. If you put a purchase on the card, make sure you have enough in savings to cover it when you pay the bill.

3. Avoid installment loans, "easy credit," and finance companies that target people with poor credit ratings. You'll pay through the nose on finance charges.

4. Pay yourself before you pay your creditors. If you have a debt you want to pay off, split your payment between short- and long-term savings and the debt itself. Make sure at least half of what you're paying goes into your pot first.

Need Help with Your Credit?
The following services can help you repay your debts and rebuild your credit if you are in trouble:

> **National Foundation for Consumer Credit, www.nfcc.org, 800-388-2227.** They can locate a consumer credit counseling service near you.

> **Debt Counselors of America, getoutofdebt.org, 800-680-3328.** This Internet-based service will connect you to a debt counselor.

> **Consolidated Credit Counseling Service, www.debtfree.org, 800-728-3632.** Similar to NFCC, a service that provides credit counseling.

Small Things Add Up:
Yet More Ways to Save

Once you've covered the "big boys" in my Triple S (Simple Super Savings) plan, you can move on to smaller-cost items. These little buggers really add up over time, so here's a few examples on how you can divert this money into your New Prosperity fund:

- **Eat out less.** I love to eat out, but I know when it gets to be too much. Here are sample benefits of saving on restaurants: If you can save just $100 a month ($25 a week), that's $1,200 a year. At 6% return, you're looking at $14,507 in 10 years or $67,958 by age 65 in a tax-deferred account (starting at age 40).
- **Buy fewer new clothes.** So many temptations—with fashions changing all the time and malls and beautiful models beckoning to us. Let's say you are a modest clothes buyer and you spend $600 a year on clothes. I know this is toward the low end of clothes-horsing, but that modest sum will be worth $33,979 in a tax-deferred account at age 65.
- **Take fewer costly vacations.** Travel can be expensive, especially to places where you have to take a plane, stay in a hotel, and eat in restaurants. There's nothing wrong with a pleasant vacation now and

again, but several vacations a year starts robbing your future. Let's say you spend $1,800 a year on trips, which is one weeklong trip in Orlando or Las Vegas and maybe a shorter trip to San Francisco or New York. Of course, one cruise could cost this much, or you could easily spend as much on a high-end resort in a few days, but for the sake of argument, let's say you average $150 a month on (nonbusiness) travel. This is travel you pay for out of pocket. That $1,800 is worth $21,760 in ten years at 6%, but blossoms to $101,937 in a tax-deferred account by age 65. I'm not saying you should pitch a tent everywhere you go, but knocking off one expensive trip or traveling locally can mean a lot down the road.

▪ **Spend less on entertainment.** I've always been crazy about movies. I even took some classes in filmmaking (anyone want to see my screenplays?). I want to see every big film and every artsy film. It will not surprise you that this penchant for entertainment can really add up over time. By the time you've paid $25 for two tickets, some popcorn, and drinks, pay the baby-sitter and go to dinner, you're looking at a $100 evening *just to see a movie*. A few times we've paid the baby-sitter more than we've paid for the actual entertainment. So let's say you save $125, which is about one night out and a few videos. That sum over ten years is worth $1,500 a year or $18,133 in ten years (that's about a year at a state college now). At age 65, that's $84,948 at that paltry 6% rate of return. Everything comes out on video now. Stay at home and yell at the screen as much as you want, eat your own popcorn, and drink your own drinks.

▪ **Cancel cable or satellite TV.** Unless you skipped the homily in this chapter on TV, you already know how I feel about television. I don't believe in paying for it. Not when there are so many great films, documentaries, and children's programs on video. You can take them out free in most public libraries. What if you could live without cable or satellite TV? That $45 a month is $540 a year. You can fund an Education IRA for your child with $500 a year, so you're seeding an education. In ten years, you have $6,528, or the downpayment on a vehicle. At age 65, you have $30,581 in a tax-deferred account or enough to *pay cash* for a basic luxury car when your body will really appreciate the comfort.

■ **Bring your lunch to work.** I really need to leave my work environment once a day, and usually that means going out to lunch. I spend about $50 a week maximum on this luxury. What if I save $10 a week by bringing in my lunch? That's $520 a year or $5,926 in ten years at 6%. That's a whole living room of furniture. Combine that with avoiding buying your coffee at a coffee shop every day at $2.50 a day—or $234 a year—and you'll have $2,667 in 10 years.

The Short List for Saving

This is a challenge to create your own savings out of "found money" that you don't need to spend. Save receipts for everything you buy in a month. Look at your checking account register and credit card bills, then total:

1. Things you spent money on you could easily live without
2. Things you gained little value from

This is your short list for ways to save. Are you still hard-pressed to find some ways to save? Here are some other ideas that are commonly ignored.

Automated teller machine fees. If you pay $1 a transaction twice a week for a year that's $104. Choose a bank that either has an ATM near you—and won't charge you an ATM fee—or write checks, free.

Eliminate costly addictions. This is an easy one to identify, but a hard one to cure. Say you buy a pack of cigarettes every week for $4.50. That's $234 a year. The same goes for a six-pack of beer every week at $2.99. That's $155.48. I'm not saying that total abstinence is possible for everybody. I buy one bottle of good vodka that lasts the summer and one bottle of cognac that lasts the winter. A have a cigar about twice a year. I enjoy them so much more that way and don't spend that much enjoying them.

Exercise at home or in your community. I never quite understood why people paid more than $800 a year to be members of health clubs when they could walk, run, or climb stairs for free. You'll be healthier, lose weight—and save money. Paying high greens fees for golf is even more perplexing, when there are so many great public and forest preserve courses. And when you rent a cart, you don't get any exercise.

Don't pay too much for insurance. Agents will implore you to buy "full coverage" for everything. You don't need it if you have short-term savings. Instead of the insurance company investing *your* money and making money for a corporation, you can invest it and make money for yourself. The simple rule is get the highest deductible—the amount of money you pay out of pocket on a claim—that you can afford. This applies to the comprehensive and collision parts of your auto insurance; your homeowners/renter's insurance and even health insurance if you are self-employed or without group coverage. The higher the deductible, the lower your premium. When it comes to life insurance, you only need it if you have dependents at home who would have no other significant means of support if you die. Buy term life at the lowest possible premium (see Resources at the end of the book for quote services).

Update your home with energy-efficient appliances. If you're in a "replacement mode" with appliances, find the most energy-efficient units you can afford. The most energy-stingy appliances carry an "Energy Star" label from the U.S. Department of Energy, and all major appliances must carry yellow "Energy" tags that show how much energy they consume in a year. Let's say you have an old, 65%-energy-efficient furnace and need to replace it. Go with a 95%-efficient furnace and you'll save $351 on a yearly bill of $1,300, according to the American Council of Energy-Efficient Economies. That's a 14% return on investment. If you're remodeling, plug up drafts; add more insulation to the walls and ceiling; insulate your water heater; replace windows with gas-filled panes; clean your furnace every year; and replace incandescent bulbs with compact fluorescents. Depending on what you do, you can save from 10% to 50% on your yearly energy bills.

Buy energy-efficient vehicles. There's no coincidence that gas-stingy vehicles are generally low priced. The more the vehicle weighs, the worse the mileage and the more fuel it uses. Not only will your cost of operation be lower with a "greener" vehicle, you'll pay it off sooner and be kinder to the environment. The following is a short list of green cars under $20,000.

GREEN CARS SAVE GREEN

Vehicle	MPG/City	MPG/Highway	Size
Honda Insight	61	70	Subcompact
Honda Civic HX	34	38	Subcompact
Toyota Echo	31	38	Subcompact
Saturn SW	27	36	Compact
Dodge Caravan	20	26	Minivan
Toyota Tacoma	21	24	Light pickup
Jeep Cherokee	18	23	Sport Utility

Source: American Council for an Energy-Efficient Economy Green Book, www.greenercars.com/gc2000.html.

A Savings Ethic from the Mahatma

Researching various ways to save has led me back to unexpected sources. One of them was Mohandas Gandhi, who was influenced by John Ruskin, the nineteenth-century critic and author. Gandhi, who helped create the planet's most populous democracy, lived a spartan life. His secret: renounce material things and enjoy your life. He found joy in simple living, simple arts, and the company of people. It would be nearly impossible for most of us to live like Gandhi, but his message was elegantly interpreted recently by environmental writer Bill McKibben:

Renunciation seems like such a joyless word. But remember Gandhi's secret for living was "renounce and enjoy." Here is the secret reason that some people in the rich world have begun to get rid of some of their stuff, move to smaller homes, eat lower on the food chain, ride bikes, reduce their expenses and scale back their careers: If you can simplify your life—and it requires a certain minimal affluence to do so—then you can have more fun than your neighbors.

It would be difficult for most of us to walk around in loincloths and regularly fast the way the Mahatma did in his life. The theme that Gandhi and other critics of Western society have explored is that what we want is not simply a quality *lifestyle,* but a higher *quality of life.* As Arne Naess, the father of "deep ecology" writes, "When circumstances force people with a high quality of life to retreat to a mere high standard [of living], the transition can be painful and dangerous for their self-respect."

So we lose something when we subscribe to the higher lifestyle that's so often oversold as the American Dream. We can save ourselves and our families. The key is savings itself.

SUMMARY

1. Understand how advertising and marketing make you spend more and save less.
2. Review your mortgage situation and choose a strategy on how to save money long term.
3. Review your transportation budget and see how you can save short term.
4. See how you can reduce your short-term debt today.
5. Create a short list of ways to save. With the money you save, proceed to the next chapter and collect $200 to start your New Prosperity fund. (Pay yourself first.)

CHAPTER 3

Creating Your Own
Investment Club

*It is more easy to write on money than to obtain it; and those who
gain it, jest much at those who only know how to write about it.*
—Voltaire, *Philosophical Dictionary*

I couldn't agree more with Monsieur Voltaire, except to note that
he's never been to a Pittsburgh investors' fair, where there are thousands of stories of people who could write books on investing. To
be precise, there are 3,441 investors in 357 clubs who could write
the book on how investing in stocks works through investment
clubs. This is hardly a jest. At least the joke was on me as I traveled
to deliver a keynote speech, sign a few books, and visit with the
investing sages of beautiful Allegheny County.

Pittsburgh is a verdant city cradled by mountains that couch the
Ohio and Monongahela rivers. It used to be a powerhouse of a city,
famous for its billowing steel mills and hundreds of train lines,
hauling everything from coal to cold-rolled coils of steel. The Pittsburgh Steelers and Pirates epitomized this blue-collar mecca with
their tough play and journeymen ethics.

Now Pittsburgh is even more beautiful. The mountains and rivers
are still there, but the air and water are much cleaner. Although far
too many mills have shut down, other, cleaner industries have taken
their places and the city has become a center for high technology.

Ed Thornblade and Dave Bigley are champions in their own right. Their Laurel Investment Club won the Pittsburgh area's title for one of the best-returning stock-investment club records. Ed, a dentist, and Dave, an optometrist, are typical investment clubbers. They have been a part of investment clubs for decades, have made a few mistakes along the way, and are investing on their own with their families.

Ed's son is investing his way through medical school and won't be saddled with a six-figure debt when he graduates. Dave's son is also in college and has been investing since he was fourteen. Like most investment clubbers, stock investing has become a family affair and a way to a certain kind of independence, and like most investment clubs, the Laurel has focused on holding stocks for long periods of time, but it wasn't always a profitable affair. Started in May 1979—during the end of a dismal period for the stock market—Ed recalls the club losing money in 1980 and 1984. The original club members bought and sold stocks at will, and even held stocks as short as one week.

Today, having ironed out a few of the kinks, the 29-member club is sitting on a $1 million portfolio. It all started with member contributions of $30 a month. Some six members don't even come to the meeting, they just send in their money. The all-male club relies upon eight men to do most of the research, but that's fine with the rest of the membership.

"We don't go into something [buying stocks] with the idea of being greedy," Ed says. "That would poison the club. Nobody is obsessed with money."

The Laurel members pick their stocks using a method developed by the National Association of Investors Corporation (a condensed version is in chapter 6) and the bottom line is always finding a well-managed company with at least 15% earnings growth per year. At that rate, a stock will double in about five years.

Having dumped stocks that don't perform, the club has sold 68 stocks in 20 years. The companies they buy are well established, and they won't even consider a company without at least five years of earnings.

"Learning is the main thing," Ed notes of the club's mission. "Now we are learning to make money."

"And we can compound our earnings and still remain conservative," Dave adds. "We are slow to do things, but our success brings a satisfaction that we can impart to our kids."

The Laurel Club provides a social setting for learning about investing. Although they had a rough few years, the club is well on its way to building wealth for families. Their portfolio represents a small cross-section of the U.S. economy, although it tends to concentrate on established technology companies. Here's how their successful portfolio looks:

THE LAUREL INVESTMENT CLUB PORTFOLIO

Technology stocks: ADC Telecom, Applied Materials, Electrosource I, GE, Nokia, Oracle, Thermo Electron

Food Service: Coca-Cola, Pepsico, Tricon Global, Wendy's International

Drugs: Merck

Retail: Wal-Mart

Other: Disney, RPM

It is surprisingly simple to build a portfolio like the Laurel's. They have bought into their stocks at low costs. For example, the average cost per share for their largest holding—GE, 1,580 shares—is a paltry $12.89. GE was selling for more than $100 a share at time of publication. Laurel's method is common to every investment club: They take their time finding long-term growth companies and reinvest dividends. The key is a social environment that overcomes members' fears of investing on their own. It's a revolution that you can take part of in building your New Prosperity.

Join the Club and the Money Revolution

I have this revolutionary theory about money. I call it Money Avoidance Dysfunction (MAD). People who suffer from this debilitating neurosis can't talk about money; they keep their money problems to themselves and stay awake nights thinking about them. They project their anxieties onto their spouses and loved ones. As a result, all of their relationships suffer. MAD makes them *mad*. They know they may not be able to retire when they want to, can't pay for their kids' college educations and ultimately are working two or three jobs to pay the bills, which are largely nondeductible debts. They are falling behind, not getting ahead. All because they don't know the psychological power of money and their relationship to it. As a result, their personal ecology is imbalanced and suffers needlessly.

Fortunately, I think that the first decade of this century will mark the beginning of the "money revolution," when a large number of people in the Northern Hemisphere awaken to what money is and what it can do for them. Money in and of itself is not a personal or private form of power. You can be the richest person in the world and sit in a room full of money and it will have *no impact* on the workings of the universe. In fact, money by itself has no power at all. It's merely a symbolic transaction of life energy. In exchange for your labor, you get a paycheck, health insurance, and a few other perks like free coffee and some paid time off. When the masses wake up and realize this—and conclude that the power of money can't be harnessed by either capitalism or Marxism—we will see a revolution akin to the Renaissance, the Scientific Revolution, and the Enlightenment combined.

What will happen during the coming money revolution? People will openly discuss losing money on bad investments and stupid market-timing decisions (buy high, don't sell dogs, don't hold long-term winners). There will be more discussion about money and its upside and downside than at any other time in history. Governments will realize that they shouldn't be in the lending business, that they are in the social investment business. People will have parties celebrating the social and spiritual relevance of money and not simply what it can buy. The unraveling of the Money Avoidance Dysfunction on a massive scale will be to economics and markets what the sexual revolution was to bedrooms. But this revolution will not be televised, to quote Gil Scott-Heron. It will be fomented on kitchen tables in modest suburban homes with picket fences, dogs in the backyard, and two cars in the garage. To some degree, this has happened all over the world, but it has yet to take hold in most middle-income households.

Let the Revolution Begin

The first phase of this money revolution has been brewing for some time in investment clubs.

Investment clubs employ a unique form of group therapy that cures MAD—if practiced regularly. Stocks are researched, discussed, and then bought for long periods of time, sometimes held up to twenty years or more. Members, however, don't need to pay a psychiatrist $200 an hour. Most clubs start out with dues of $25 a month, which is invested in carefully selected stocks.

INVESTMENT CLUBS: A PROFILE

- There are more than 650,000 members of NAIC investment clubs
- There are 36,500 clubs nationwide
- The average personal member portfolio value is $243,666
- There are an average 16 members per club
- An average $58 is invested per member per month
- 67.9% of NAIC investment club members are female
- Men-only clubs tend to trade more than women-only clubs (which outperform their male-only counterparts) and have lower returns as a result. Mixed-gender clubs have the highest returns.

Source: www.naicmedia.com. National Association of Investors Corporation, Madison Heights, Michigan.

A Brief History of Investment Clubs

The history of investment clubs is a bit elusive, but some have been around for a long time. How long, nobody is quite sure, but the unofficial start was just during and after World War II when a small group of soldiers and veterans started the Mutual Investment Club in Detroit, pooling their money to buy stocks. Since then, more than one million people have joined investment clubs, although you'll never see coverage of them in the *Wall Street Journal, Barron's, New York Times,* CNBC, thestreet.com, or on the nightly news. The institutions we know as Wall Street and the financial media don't really care about investment clubs because they are not sexy and involve no high-paid analysts or high-flying brokers. Clubs buy and hold stocks based on solid research, not fads or hot tips. They discuss their investments openly and are honest about their mistakes. They avoid brokers and the "conventional wisdom on Wall Street." And, oh yes, they make money consistently, but don't brag about it.

Since clubs are essentially set up to educate their partners, they have no interest in plugging hot companies, nor are they watching stock tickers all day long. In short, investment clubbers have a healthy mental attitude toward money and know they won't make a killing overnight. That's a big part of the money revolution. They don't sweat their investments and they do everything the opposite of Wall Street. On Main Street, things happen a little differently and it works over time.

The reason clubs promote healthy money psychology is that they are not afraid to fail. By and large, investment clubbers are not educated stock pickers; they learn by doing. They don't have Ivy League finance degrees or MBAs and they span the gamut from electrical engineers to sanitation engineers.

How to Start a Club

Even if you have an investment club of one, here's what you'll need to start:

- A willingness to learn something new about investing on a consistent basis
- A willingness to invest at least $10 a month
- A willingness to do this over time by buying a portfolio of stocks and reinvesting dividends
- A willingness to make mistakes and learn from them

Start with yourself as a club of one. You can join as many clubs as you have time for, but start with your own money. Admit to yourself that despite your feelings about money, they can all be overcome and you can make money investing by learning how to do it. It's not complicated and it's not a gift to certain people. As so many gurus have said, "The power is within." So it wouldn't hurt to start a club of one, or with your significant other.

Part of the therapy of defeating MAD is that you make affirmations by yourself and in public. "My name is John and I am afraid to deal with money, but I will learn how to manage it." Say this. Write it down. I once had a problem with money—I didn't have any. So I decided to learn how to save. Then I progressed to investing when I figured out that inflation was eating up my savings. I talked about it. I asked my father what he did. I read books. I have degrees in psychology and communications, so I knew about as much about money as a squirrel knows about calculus. Joining a club, however, got me started on the road to enlightenment.

There are some beautiful side benefits to investment clubbing:

- If your spouse, significant other, or family members are involved, you are all on the same level. You all have to do some research and succeed or fail based on your work. This is the great equalizer in investing.
- You will be able to discuss money transactions with a diverse group of people, sometimes complete strangers. This is healthy. If you can talk to strangers about money, you can certainly talk to yourself about money.

KITCHEN-TABLE TIP

SEED MONEY FOR YOUR INVESTMENT CLUB

Sit down at your favorite informal eating place. Save some receipts for a week, throw them on the table on Saturday. If you're like most working people, you like to go out to lunch and buy some coffee. Say you spend $6 per day on lunch and $2.50 on a double latte. That's $42.50 a week or $2,040 per year based on a 240-day working year. That's enough to fund an IRA or your investment club @ $170 a month. Of course, you can start with as little as $10 a month, but "finding" the money will seed your club.

- You will certainly not be distracted by what the market does that day or week. You are buying for the long term in small amounts. Nobody gets devastated by holding big positions on margin in stocks that get creamed in market routs. Easy does it.
- Clubs are great for balancing your personal ecology. Because you have a sustainable attitude about money—you do it gently on a regular basis—the rest of your life may even out. You will eventually be able to work less, spend more time with your family, travel, and do the things you want. All because you tackled your fears about investing.

How to Find Club Members and Hold That First Meeting

Without a doubt, the organizing is the fun part. To be honest, as a journalist I seldom actively participate in what I'm writing about. After all, us ink-stained wretches can't get too close to a subject. It may impair our precious objectivity. So when I finished *The Investment Club Book,* Kathleen somewhat surprised me by saying, "Why don't we start an investment club?" Well, as someone who had just written *the book* on the subject, I was confident that we would prosper and pick some dynamite stocks and be able to retire early. Not only that, but the family members we recruited would "be on the pig's back" (a strange Irish expression for good fortune) as well.

Kathleen's mother and father came on board and started to learn how to pick stocks. At first, it was rough going, but they eventually decided to contribute dues. Then there was her brother Martin, who had just gotten married and was learning about investing. Kathleen's other brother, Steven, also joined, with his wife, Maria. Nobody from my side of the family was interested although my father was already in an investment club. By the end of our first year, despite all of our good intentions at educating everyone at a moderate pace, we had bought only two stocks and lost Steven and Maria. Then my in-laws Joe and Theresa dropped by the wayside to become passive investors using Martin as a proxy. Martin then went through a painful divorce, so we had to cash out his ex. By the end of our third year, we only had some four stocks with half of our membership out the door. Hardly an auspicious beginning on the road to riches. There was a reason we called ourselves the Wall Street Prowlers.

There is no ideal way to form an investment club, but be aware of a few facts of human nature: Not everyone's a "joiner," and not everyone will want to do the work to learn how to become a competent investor. Although I think it's unusual to lose half of your membership, you may see attrition of up to one-third. And you will always lose members who are just too busy or don't want to contribute in a meaningful way. There are a few guidelines you need to know when assembling a club:

1. Try to sit in on a meeting at another club before you start your own. You don't even have to join. You can just be a fly on the wall. There are several model clubs that meet in communities all across the world where you can just sit and learn at your own pace and contribute when you feel like it. Most public libraries allow them to meet there. This is an ideal starting point if you are totally squeamish about the idea.

2. If you can join an existing club, that's a gentle start. Some clubs will let you join with as little as $10 a month, although $25 a month is fairly common. Being a club member and knowing that your money is at risk puts a whole new spin on things. You see how the group dynamic works and whether it will work with the people you have in mind for your own club. Even if you are a club of one—and you will be at some point—being a part of a group makes the money experience social and engaging.

3. Recruit people you know who are sincere. You're probably familiar with the "polling effect." Whenever a totally unobjectionable question is asked, most people respond in the affirmative. "Do you want to make a million dollars?" Well, who's going to say no? It's the same thing when you ask people if they want to learn how to make money. Nearly all will say yes, but down the road you find out that from 10% to 60% of them are insincere and back out when they find out that real thinking and a small amount of work is involved. The most successful clubs are composed of people you know will remain committed.

4. Get plenty of educational materials and expertise to back you up. There's plenty of support for investment clubbers. You can obtain a mountain of materials and expertise from the National Association of Investors Corporation (NAIC) or the American Association of Individual Investors (see Resources at the end of this book). You can even have people who have started clubs advise your club for free. You're not out there alone. Get as much help as you can.

5. Go slow; remember the main objective is education. Unlike the frenetic beckoning of CNBC or Web sites that trumpet stock quotes, you don't have to buy a stock until you understand *how* to buy it. That means several meetings that are nothing but educational sessions. You don't need to proceed until you or the rest of your club is ready.

6. Make sure your membership is diverse. While women-only clubs tend to outperform all-male clubs, the best clubs have men and women. Also diversify by age, ethnicity, affiliation (mix in nonfamily members), and education. It will make for better decision making and livelier club meetings.

Your Club's Rules

Every club needs rules, or else nothing gets done and everything's helter-skelter. The rules that govern a club—which is actually an investment partnership—are called bylaws. This is sort of the constitution a club abides by, and since everybody in the club votes on the by-laws, they can only be amended by a vote.

By-laws ensure that no one person or investment philosophy dominates the club and you have set policies on monthly investments, withdrawals, and many other issues that are designed to keep things running smoothly. Keep in mind that you can have by-laws governing anything you want, but try to keep them simple.

The following by-laws are recommended as a starting point. They are largely based on the Mutual Investment Club of Detroit, which is the godfather of all postwar private investment clubs and is the model used by the National Association of Investors Corporation (see Resources for more information).

YOUR INVESTMENT CLUB

This AGREEMENT of PARTNERSHIP, effective as of _____ (date) by and between the undersigned, to wit:

　　　(names of partners)

NOW, THEREFORE IT IS AGREED:

1. Formation. The undersigned hereby form a General Partnership* in accordance with and subject to the laws of the State of _____.

2. Name. The name of the partnership shall be "Your Investment Club."

3. Term. The partnership shall begin on _____ (date) and shall continue until December 31 of the same year and thereafter from year to year unless terminated.

---

*You are establishing a taxable legal entity when you form a general partnership.

4. Purpose. The only purpose of the partnership is to invest the assets of the partnership solely in stocks for the education and benefit of the partners.*

5. Meetings. Periodic meetings shall be held as determined by the partnership.

6. Capital Contributions. The partners may make capital contributions to the partnership on the date of each meeting in such amounts as the partnership shall determine, provided, however, that no partner's capital account shall exceed twenty percent (20%) of the capital accounts of all partners.†

7. Value of the Partnership. The current value of the assets of the partnership, less the current value of the liabilities of the partnership (referred to as the "value of the partnership"), shall be determined as of a regularly scheduled date and time ("valuation date") preceding the date of each periodic meeting determined by the Club.‡

8. Capital Accounts. A capital account shall be maintained in the name of each partner. Any change in the value of the partnership on any valuation date shall be credited or debited, respectively, to each partner's capital account on that date. Any other method of valuating each partner's capital account may be substituted for this method, provided the substituted method results in exactly the same valuation as previously provided herein. Each partner's contribution to, or capital withdrawal from, the partnership shall be credited, or debited, respectively, to that partner's capital account.§

---

*You can invest in stocks, real state investment trusts, mutual funds, and bonds, but most investment clubs focus exclusively on stocks.

†You can specify a monthly amount, but that's not necessary. The 20% limit, which can be changed, is to prevent one partner from having inordinate control.

‡Your club needs to do valuation statements each month showing how much your investments are worth and how much each member's investment is worth. You can prepare the valuation statements on the same time each month (if you use software, this is a snap), or on the date of the meeting. Our club chose to do valuations on the date of the meeting to give us an up-to-date picture of the club's holdings.

§When each member gets their own capital account, they know exactly how much they have every month. This is a fair accounting system that leaves nothing to chance.

9. Management. Each partner shall participate in the management and conduct of the affairs of the partnership in proportion to his capital account. Except as otherwise determined, all decisions shall be made by the partners whose capital accounts total a majority of the value of the capital accounts of all the partners.[*]

10. Sharing of Profits and Losses. Net profits and losses of the partnership shall inure to, and be borne by, the partners, in proportion to the value of each of their capital accounts.[†]

11. Books of Account. Books of account of the transactions of the partnership shall be kept and at all times be available and open to inspection and examination by any partner.[‡]

12. Annual Accounting. Each calendar year, a full and complete account of the condition of the partnership shall be made to the partners.[§]

13. Bank Account. The partnership may select a bank for the purpose of opening a bank account. Funds in the bank account shall be withdrawn by checks signed by any partner designated by the partnership.[||]

14. Broker Account. None of the partners of this partnership shall be a broker. However, the partnership may select a broker and enter into such agreements with the broker as required for the purchase or sale of securities. Securities owned by the partnership shall be registered in the partnership name unless another name shall be designated by the partnership.[#]

Any corporation or transfer agent called upon to transfer any securities to or from the name of the partnership shall be entitled to rely on instructions or assignments signed by any

---

[*]This is a flexible clause. Many members don't participate in the club except for contributing money, which is okay in some clubs. If you allow "passive" investors, strike the first sentence.

[†]Everybody shares profits and losses according to how much of the club they own.

[‡]This keeps everyone honest since any member can see the books any time they wish.

[§]Another good idea that keeps everything open and accountable.

[||]The club designates two members who are on the bank's "signature guarantee" card. Only they can make transactions.

[#]If you keep all securities in the name of the club, that eliminates any potential conflicts.

partner without inquiry as to the authority of the person(s) signing such instructions or assignments or as to the validity of any transfer to or from the name of the partnership.*

At the time of a transfer of securities, the corporation or transfer agent is entitled to assume (1) that the partnership is still in existence and (2) that this Agreement is in full force and effect and has not been amended unless the corporation has received written notice to the contrary.

15. No Compensation. No partner shall be compensated for services rendered to the partnership, except reimbursement for expenses.†

16. Additional Partners. Additional partners may be admitted at any time, upon the unanimous consent of the partners, so long as the number of partners does not exceed (X).‡

16A. Transfers to a Trust. A partner may, after giving written notice to the other partners, transfer his interest in the partnership to a revocable living trust of which he is the grantor and sole trustee.§

16B. Removal of a Partner. Any partner may be removed by agreement of the partners whose capital accounts total a majority of the value of all partners' capital accounts. Written notice of a meeting where removal of a partner is to be considered shall include a specific reference to this matter. The removal shall become effective upon payment of the value of the removed partner's capital account, which shall be in accordance with the provisions on full withdrawal of a partner noted in paragraphs 18 and 20. The vote action shall be treated as receipt of request for withdrawal.‖

17. Termination of Partnership. The partnership may be terminated by agreement of the partners whose capital

---

*Those assigned to handle stock transactions act as secretaries or treasurers of the club.
†You're all volunteers for your own benefit. Nobody gets a salary. You're in the club to learn first, then make money through investing.
‡You can limit the size of your club.
§If your members have "living trusts," then they can assign their interests to a trust.
‖Majority rules if you want to dump a partner.

accounts total a majority in value of the capital accounts of all the partners. Written notice of a meeting where termination of the partnership is to be considered shall include a specific reference to this matter. The partnership shall terminate upon a majority vote of all partners' capital accounts. Written notice of the decision to terminate the partnership shall be given to all the partners. Payment shall then be made of all the liabilities of the partnership and a final distribution of the remaining assets, either in cash or in kind, shall promptly be made to the partners or their personal representatives in proportion to each partner's capital account.[*]

18. Voluntary Withdrawal (Partial or Full) of a Partner. Any partner may withdraw a part or all of the value of his capital account in the partnership and the partnership shall continue as a taxable entity. The partner withdrawing a part or all of the value of his capital account shall give notice of such intention in writing to the Secretary. Written notice shall be deemed to be received as of the first meeting of the partnership at which it is presented. If written notice is received between meetings it will be treated as received at the first following meeting.[†]

In making payment, the value of the partnership, as set forth in the valuation statement prepared for the first meeting following the meeting at which notice is received from a partner requesting a partial or full withdrawal, will be used to determine the value of the partner's account.

> The partnership shall pay the partner who is withdrawing a portion or all of the value of his capital account in the partnership in accordance with paragraph 20 of this Agreement.

---

[*]Since a partnership is a legal entity, you have to vote to dissolve it and clear the books of any liabilities.

[†]You have to give written notice if you want to take your money out. There should be a time between when the request is received and when the club cuts a check.

19. Death or Incapacity of a Partner. In the event of the death or incapacity of a partner (or the death or incapacity of the grantor and sole trustee of a revocable living trust, if such trust is partner pursuant to Paragraph 16A hereof), receipt of notice shall be treated as a notice of full withdrawal.

20. Terms of Payment. In the case of a partial withdrawal, payment may be made in cash or securities of the partnership or a mix of each at the option of the partner making the partial withdrawal. In the case of a full withdrawal, payment may be made in cash or securities or a mix of each at the option of the remaining partners. In either case, where securities are to be distributed, the remaining partners select the securities.

Where cash is transferred, the partnership shall transfer to the partner (or other appropriate entity) withdrawing a portion or all of his interest in the partnership, an amount equal to the lesser of (i) ninety-seven percent (97%) of the value of the capital account being withdrawn, or (ii) the value of the capital account being withdrawn, less the actual cost to the partnership of selling securities to obtain cash to meet the withdrawal. The amount being withdrawn shall be paid within 10 days after the valuation date used in determining the withdrawal amount.

If the partner withdrawing a portion or all of the value of his capital account in the partnership desires an immediate payment in cash, the partnership at its earliest convenience may pay eighty percent (80%) of the estimated value of his capital account and settle the balance in accordance with the valuation and payment procedures set forth in paragraphs 18 and 20.

Where securities are transferred, the partnership shall select securities to transfer equal to the value of the capital account or a portion of the capital account being withdrawn (i.e., without a reduction for broker commissions). Securities shall be transferred as of the date of the club's valuation statement prepared to determine the value of that partner's capital account in the partnership. The Club's broker shall be advised that ownership of the securities has been transferred to the partner as of the valuation date used for the withdrawal.*

21. Forbidden Acts: No partner shall:

(a) Have the right or authority to bind or obligate the partnership to any extent whatsoever with regard to any matter outside the scope of the partnership purpose.

(b) Except as provided in paragraph 16A, without the unanimous consent of all the other partners, assign, transfer, pledge, mortgage, or sell all or part of his interest in the partnership to any other partner or other person whomsoever, or enter into any agreement as the result of which any person or persons not a partner shall become interested with him in the partnership.

(c) Purchase an investment for the partnership where less than the full purchase price is paid for same.

(d) Use the partnership name, credit, or property for other than partnership purposes.

(e) Do any act detrimental to the interests of the partnership or which would make it impossible to carry on the business or affairs of the partnership.†

This Agreement of Partnership shall be binding upon the respective heirs, executors, administrators, and personal representatives of the partners. The partners have caused this Agreement of Partnership to be executed on the dates indicated below, effective as of the date indicated above.

Partners: [Everyone signs after a vote is taken on the by-laws.]

---

*This gets complicated, but the basic rule is that the club wants to provide disincentives for withdrawing money. In this example, the club takes 3% for transactions costs, but it can be higher if your club decides to keep more.

†These are the "safety clauses." This forbids members from signing up for phony real estate deals and acting irresponsibly.

Resources You'll Need for Club Education

Some of your best educational materials will be free and come from your public library. Even if you are on your own, you can avail yourself of the following resources:

- **Value Line Investment Survey.** For most investment clubbers, *Value Line* is the first line of defense when picking a stock. The venerable publication, found in the business reference section of almost every library, rates stocks, predicts where the company is going, and is a treasure trove of valuable information on "financials."
- **Morningstar.** There are several components of Morningstar Inc., a great deal of which can be found on their unique Web site at www.morningstar.com. They are famous for their evaluations of mutual funds, although they also do analysis of individual stocks. Both are great resources that are always improving.
- **NAIC,** www.better-investing.org, 248-583-6242. As the umbrella educational organization for most investment clubs, NAIC is the mother lode for investment club information. They provide everything from start-up materials to club accounting software. While you may not subscribe to their way of doing things, everything from their magazine (*Better Investing*) to their valuation software will make your club run a lot more smoothly.
- **Quicken.com,** www.quicken.com. The Quicken megasite has dozens of components. You can get basic stock quotes and financials. You can also get analysts' reports and use any one of several financial calculators. A most reliable third resource.
- **Investorama,** www.investorama.com. An online community with huge archives on anything relating to investment clubs.
- ***Standard & Poor's.*** The *S&P Reports* do much of what *Value Line* does, though more in the context of a specific industry. S&P provides financials and industry overviews and is a solid backup to whatever *Value Line* provides.

Getting Your Club Running: The First Year

Let's assume you now have members. They are so eager to learn about investing that they are champing at the bit. They are ready to devour the nonmystical, easy-to-comprehend ways of making money at stocks long term. They have stopped buying lottery tickets and are ready to contribute at least $10 a month toward this effort. They are willing to go to the library or search the Internet for information on stocks. Let's review how your club should be moving along.

Decide on a monthly contribution and meeting date. Before you pick your first stock, you'll need the cash to make purchases down the road. It's a simple decision. While $25 is a popular monthly amount, $10 is certainly acceptable. You'll need a few months to build up your kitty before you can buy shares. Another major detail in the first meetings is to establish a regular meeting date. Everyone has ongoing commitments, but once you lock in a meeting date, members will tend to stick to it and you won't have to worry about attendance. If you can't agree to a regular meeting date or place, then everything else will become extremely difficult.

Pick a name. Finally, something fun to do. You shouldn't spend a lot of time on this since you'll need to call yourself something to open a checking, money market, or brokerage account. This is a surprisingly contentious process that will generate many ideas and a little rancor if your choice for a name isn't picked. Get a name from each member and then take a vote.

Pick a broker and set up a checking/money market account. You'll need a place to put the money (see next chapter for details). Nearly every brokerage account has a money market account attached to it. That means that cash that isn't invested is earning interest and you can either transfer the money or write a check when you're ready. All of your monthly contributions go into this account. Ideally, the brokerage/money market account also features low commissions and connects you directly with dividend reinvestment plans (DRIP), which automatically invest dividends and allow you to buy new shares without paying a commission. All brokers can transfer shares into DRIPs if the shares are bought in the name of your club and not the broker's "street name." Always register shares in the name of your club and not an individual. You can then have a checking account or money market account in the club's name and keep your cash available for purchases. The treasurer and secretary need to obtain literature on brokers and account fees and present it to the club by the second meeting. The club can then vote on the broker account that suits their needs. The treasurer will then assume the responsibility of keeping the account balances of the broker account and reporting on balances every month.

EASY WAYS OF PICKING A BROKER

Although there are hundreds of brokers out there, it is a simple matter to pick one. Get the one with the lowest commissions and the best service. I know, this is easier said than done. Brokering these days, however, is an extremely competitive business. Not only are commissions next to nothing, but you can even find a broker who will waive commissions entirely. Here's what to do:

1. Shop the Internet, business section of your newspaper, or *Barron's*. That's where brokers advertise. Plug in "discount brokers" in your Internet search engine. See who has the lowest commissions and the easiest terms. Also check the brokers section of www.gomezadvisors.com or www.smartmoney.com.
2. Check the minimum account balance requirements. Many brokers will want you to have several thousand dollars in cash or securities to get you going. For your club, the lower the minimum, the better.
3. Do they offer dividend reinvestment? Many brokers claim to offer this service, but it's little more than a smokescreen. Modern brokers pair a legitimate DRIP service with low rates.
4. Whose name will be on the account? Your club secretary and treasurer should be authorized to make trades.

PLACES TO START WHEN LOOKING FOR BROKERS

The following are some inexpensive, Internet-based brokers. There are more brokers listed in Resources at the end of the book.

BuyandHold, www.buyandhold.com. This broker pairs a dividend reinvestment service with a discount brokerage.

Financial Cafe, www.thefinancialcafe.com. A broker that offers "free trades" at market price, other trades at $16.95. No account minimum.

Freetrade, www.freetrade.com. With a minimum $5,000 balance, market orders are free.

Netstock Direct, www.netstockdirect.com. Similar to Buyand-Hold.

Have you elected capable officers? Although this seems like the first thing you need to do, elections don't always work for all clubs at the first meeting. You'll find some members are natural leaders, others are followers. Some are good with numbers—and would make good treasurers—and some are better with words and make better secretaries. See who is likely to do the work and fit them into the proper position. The lion's share of the work will be done by the treasurer, who keeps the valuation statements (how much everyone owns by member) and the books (checking, brokerage accounts, cash on hand). This person should be detail oriented and consistent. The secretary keeps the minutes and works with the treasurer to transact trades. The president makes sure the meeting runs smoothly and the vice president is sort of a "whip" to make sure research gets done and assists the other officers. All officers need to be in place by the third meeting at the latest. You can vote on officers once a year.

Does everyone know what they're supposed to be doing? Aside from the officers, everyone should be involved. It's not too much to ask every member to bring a stock for review. The secretary and treasurer may be excused while they set up the club's books and by-laws. Of course, not everyone will participate, but as a club you need to encourage it. Those members who are there to benefit from others' work need to realize that they won't learn anything until they go through the process of picking, analyzing, and investing in stocks. After a while, if they learn their skills well, picking good stocks will become as automatic as making a weekly grocery list.

Do you have an agreement on investment philosophy? This is an informal agreement that reflects the personalities of the members. Some clubs adopt an aggressive posture and only buy technology stocks, while others stick with old-line pharmaceuticals and utilities. An investment philosophy requires some discussion and will take a few meetings to iron out. Our club, for example, will only buy stocks with a dividend reinvestment plan and several years of earnings. You need to have some philosophy that almost everyone agrees to before your first stock buy. Dissenting members are welcome to buy stocks on their own.

Have you given your by-laws a good reading? At least three meetings should do it. The first meeting involves reading over the by-laws template in this chapter and deciding what you want and don't want. Keep any language designed to protect members if there are withdrawals or unsanctioned activities. The rest is up to you. The second meeting is for discussion of the first draft of your modified by-laws, and by the third meeting you should be able to vote on them. If there are any changes, bring them up a year later in a by-law review. You can always vote to make alterations based on how your club operates.

Is everyone on the same page? Have you reviewed the details on how to pick stocks? I know this is a bit out of sync—and you'll need to read chapter 6 for specifics—but everyone needs to be familiar with the basics of stock picking before you actually present stocks for possible purchase. There will be stragglers who "just don't get it." Take your time. The market will still be there when you're ready. Remember, you are studying the process and everyone needs to be involved in that way. You're not set up to conquer the market, you're in a club to have fun and learn. Feel free to invite experienced club members to come and give instructional programs or tap in to the hundreds of materials provided by the NAIC. Even if you are on your own, study what you need to know before your first stock buy. It may take months, but laying a good foundation of knowledge will make for better decision making.

SUMMARY: GETTING YOUR CLUB TOGETHER

1. Know that you are a part of a money revolution and want to make investing a social event.
2. Decide if you want to form a club by yourself, join an existing club, or form one with people you know.
3. Recruit members who are sincere about learning about investing and who work well within the group.
4. Have a few meetings to educate members about how to pick stocks for the long term.
5. After you feel comfortable with the group and its knowledge base, draft by-laws. Get every member to read, understand, amend, and approve them.
6. Research stocks at the library or on the Internet. Have fun while you're learning.

Parking That Pays:
Great Savings Places for
Your New Prosperity Funds

Spirits and ghosts are beings in such a middling state of existence; and money is both real and not real, like a spook. We invented money and we use it, yet we cannot either understand its laws or control its actions.

—Lionel Trilling

It was a dreary day in early spring in Hegewisch, a bungalow neighborhood on the southeast side of Chicago. I was on the police beat that day, nearly twenty years ago, at my second newspaper reporting job, when a dispatch sizzled across a police scanner. A man was holding a woman hostage on a commuter train.

I hurried off with the *Daily Calumet's* perky photographer Suza Matczak to see what was happening at the station of the South Shore line, a dilapidated yet little intrepid commuter line that runs from downtown Chicago to northeast Indiana along Lake Michigan.

At the station, the Chicago police had already assessed the situation. James Roseborough, a Gary man, was holding a knife to a woman's throat. The train car had been emptied of passengers. Jill Jarnecke was on her way home from a birthday party when the crazed man took her hostage, demanding to see the mayor of Chicago and the FBI. The cops couldn't even talk to the delusional man. In Chicago, there was a protocol for dealing with that type of situation: "Take him out."

Patrolman Jesse Camerena stealthily entered the rear of the rusting steel passenger car and made his way to where Roseborough was. I heard two short, dull pops as the patrolman leapt up and shot Roseborough with his service revolver. His clean, white tennis shoes were the only thing I saw of him. The next thing I saw was the stretcher bearing Roseborough being brought off the train and loaded into a paddy wagon.

The murder of James Roseborough has never left me, although I left my newspaper job. I am still curious as to how James Roseborough came to that desperate last act. Someday I hope I will know how this single life could have been saved and what saving a life means in the context of everything else.

My life has passed through so many tunnels since then, many of them dark and sooty. I spent a great amount time of time and money in bars doing nothing in particular except drinking and wondering why I should be doing anything else. I wasn't saving anything. I was *consuming* my life, one drink at a time. It was a profligate waste of youth and I take full responsibility for it. I didn't really end this consumptive quest until I met Kathleen at a place that produced electronic information, a forerunner to the Internet. She was a computer artist. I was an editor masticating newswire copy to fit a video screen. It was a miserable and tedious job and Kathleen was my redemption.

What convinces one that life itself is worth saving? I can tell you there was at least one day in my youth when I gave it an inordinate amount of thought. At the risk of sounding vain, I'm a good example of how to recover from being an empty, sybaritic spender to a knowledgeable investor.

You'll recall the story of my father growing up in the Depression and saving every penny. Like most people of his generation, he *had* to sacrifice. As a baby boomer, I felt no such inclination. I spent everything I had up to the age of twenty-five on pizza, beer, and three years of college (I got a bachelor's degree in that time). But when I came to know how life could end in such a brief, violent

WHY 401(K) IS THE BEST DEAL

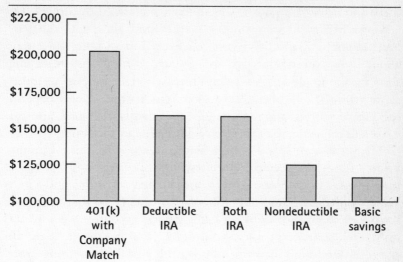

Assumptions:

- Yearly $2,000 of income invested for a period of 30 years at an 8% average annual return.
- 28% income tax and 20% capital gains tax (paid yearly for basic savings).
- Lump-sum distribution made at retirement and all taxes paid in full.
- Company-match contributions are 25% of employee contributions and are fully vested.
- This analysis does *not* rely on the common assumption that income taxes in retirement will be lower than current income taxes. If it did, the difference between the tax-deferred investments and the taxable investments would be even greater.

Source: Quicken.com.

moment, I began to save. I can't say that I found God or even stopped drinking right away, but I found a surprising vehicle that helped me save something: A money market fund.

I discovered money market funds during an ancient and troubled time in the late 1970s when interest rates and inflation were well into the double digits. It was a time when only fools went near the stock market. The Dow Jones Industrial Average was in the hundreds and real estate was the way to make money. At the time, I was getting a 14% yield on my money market fund, although that translated to about 1% return when you figured in an inflation rate of about 13%. Nevertheless, my money market fund was the staging zone for my single-guy forays into buying stereo equipment, musical instruments, and launching a local entertainment newspaper. I still have my stereo and instruments; the newspaper folded, and as I write this money market rates have descended to about 6%.

My instruments and stereo may be collecting dust, but my money fund is still earning interest and funding family-oriented savings goals like a home down payment, new furniture, and a new vehicle purchase in the next few years. I discovered that once you have a money fund, unlike a bank savings account, you can not only track short-term interest rates, but you can use it as an all-purpose warehouse for your money until you do something more interesting with your savings.

If there's one vehicle that a saver/investor of any stripe should have, it's a money market fund. This vehicle is the gas tank and battery that will drive your savings plan. Like the gas tank of a car, it needs to be replenished, doesn't need premium to run well and works automatically to feed your other investments.

How Money Funds Work

To understand how a money fund works, think of a how a vehicle starts. The engine's starter motor draws current from the battery and fuel from the gas tank to cause internal combustion in the heads of the cylinders. From there, you have some pretty consistent locomotion and you're on your way if everything else is working. A money fund provides energy storage as well, in the form of cash. Here's how it works:

Money funds pool capital in the form of short-term debt securities. "General purpose" money funds buy anything from three-to six-month U.S. Treasury bills to commercial paper, banker's acceptance notes, and even Eurodollar certificates of deposit. Generally, the maturity on these notes is no more than one year, so there's little risk you'll lose principal.

Money fund values stay at $1 per share all the time, but yields reflect short-term interest rates. Unlike bonds, money fund values remain the same when rates rise and fall. Yields—interest on your holdings—rise and fall accordingly.

Money funds come in many forms. "Government-only" money funds invest in U.S. government obligations. "Tax-free" money funds are exempt from federal—and often state—income taxes because they invest in securities issued by tax-exempt bodies.

Money funds are diversified and safe. There's only been one case in which money funds actually lost value since their inception in 1972. If you want the government-insured version of money funds, invest in a money market deposit account (MMDA), which is offered by banks and thrifts and carries federal deposit insurance against default. You will, however, reap a higher yield by the noninsured—but safe—money market mutual funds.

Immediate redemption is available from money funds. Money funds allow check writing, wire transfers, or transfers into other mutual funds. They are liquid, meaning you can get your money out any time without penalty. That's why they are instrumental as holding places for cash.

Management expenses are often waived on money funds. Like most mutual funds, money funds generally charge you an annual percentage (based on the amount invested) to manage your funds. Since there are more than 1,300 money funds in this competitive business, however, you can find funds that waive this annual expense, which results in a higher yield.

KITCHEN-TABLE TIP

MONEY FOR YOUR MONEY MARKET FUND

One of the best ways of funding a money market fund is to deposit your salary raises, tax refunds, extra paychecks, and bonuses into your money fund. If you pay off a loan or credit card, write a check for the same amount you would have written to your creditors and deposit it in the money fund.

How to Use a Money Fund

Use a money fund as a place to hold your funds for short-term needs and investing long term. Once you set one up with a mutual fund or brokerage house, do the following:

1. Set up an automatic transfer from either your checking account or payroll. If your employer has direct deposit, have your paycheck deposited directly into your money fund. This strategy ensures that every dollar is earning interest from the second it's wired from your employer. Every mutual fund company can do this. All you have to do is fill out a one-page form.

2. To pay bills, have your money fund transfer the amount into your checking account to cover your monthly expenses, or write checks directly from your money fund. Just keep in mind that many money funds require a minimum check amount, so that may not be a suitable arrangement for paying small bills. You can set up automatic withdrawal for your big bills (mortgage/rent, car payments) directly from your money fund.

3. Use your money fund as a staging area for long-term investing. You can pool money there for investing in your Individual Retirement Accounts (IRAs), Education IRAs, small company plans (SEP-IRAs, SIMPLEs), stock dividend reinvestment plans or other mutual funds. You can set up automatic withdrawal of a set amount every month into the funds and stocks of your choice, or you can just write a check when you have the money to invest.

Money Fund Fine Print:
What You Need to Know

Although money funds are flexible vehicles for pooling your money, you need to sort through some details to see which one is right for you. Here's what you need to know:

What is the minimum initial investment? This is a huge range—from $500 to $25,000. It's generally not true that the more money you have on deposit the better the yield, although that's true with some funds. Pick a fund that can accommodate what you can afford to deposit.

What is the minimum "subsequent" investment and check amount? If you're planning to use your money fund to pay monthly bills and the minimum check amount is $250, then you may have the wrong fund for your needs. Funds with the greatest flexibility have low thresholds for investments and check writing.

- **Exchanges.** Most mutual fund "families" allow a free transfer or "exchange" into their other funds. You can write a check to any party or fund; this is simply a common convenience.
- **Free checks.** It's fairly common for money funds to provide unlimited numbers of checks free. Ask or consult the fund literature to make sure.
- **Telephone redemption.** This can be used to redeem all or some of your shares or to wire the funds to another account.
- **Expenses.** Due to the competition in the fund business, you can easily find one that charges no annual expenses for management and administration. A fund that waives expenses should be your first choice. If you find a fund that offers the combination of features you need (see above), then check into the fund's annual "expense ratio," which is the percentage of your assets taken by the fund company for management and administration. According to *IBC Money Fund Report,* the average range for money fund expense ratios is from 0.6% to 0.7% per year. Of course, the lower the expense ratio the better. Avoid any money

fund that levies a "12-b-1" charge, which is basically a fee (they charge to you) for marketing the fund. It's like a car dealer adding on $100 to a car invoice so that he can advertise it to others.

- **Cash management accounts.** Also called "central asset accounts," these all-in-one vehicles combine brokerage accounts, money funds, credit cards, checking, and a host of financial services. Any funds not invested in stocks, funds, bonds, options, or futures is automatically "swept" into the money fund by the company offering the service. These accounts often have fairly high minimum investments and annual fees. They are worth it only if the other services included are discounted and you will use them on a regular basis.

Putting Your Money Fund to Work

A money market account or fund is like a battery. In order for it to perform over time, it needs to be recharged. It doesn't grow by itself and only produces a small yield, so to make it useful you need to recharge it with fresh cash on a regular basis. The best use of a money market account, as we've discussed, is as a holding place, a warehouse for funds to be used for investing. In order to make the most efficient use of this vehicle, you need to earmark two kinds of money:

1. Short-term savings. This is cash you need to preserve for a major purchase, or several smaller ones, in the next five years or so. Major purchases would include a down payment for a house, a vehicle, furniture, or major home repairs/remodeling. How much you set aside depends on the scope of what you're buying. If you're saving up for a house, it's prudent to put down 20% of the purchase price plus a few thousand for closing, moving, and other related expenses. So, for a $200,000 house, set aside $42,000 to $45,000 and you're covered. It's good to have a few thousand to cover major home items like a water heater, furnace, roof, and modest repairs. You should have a good idea of the age of your appliances and what needs to be replaced when. Remodeling needs to be budgeted carefully. Minor bathroom remodeling jobs run up to $5,000; $10,000 for a complete overhaul with new fixtures, floor, and tile. A kitchen is a sky's-the-limit project, but a modest remodeling will run at least $10,000, which would not include new flooring. In any case, get several estimates and save up what you need in your short-term savings. To get a little better yield on your short-term savings, go into intermediate-term Treasury notes (see next section).

2. Long-term savings. This is basically retirement/college tuition money (unless you're less than five years away from the first college bills). In this instance, money shouldn't stay in your money fund for a long period of time. Set up the account as a receptacle to hold the money until another investment company can receive it. Here's how that works: Earmark money deposited in your money fund for funding your Roth, conventional IRA, or SEP-IRA. Buy individual stocks through reinvestment plans. The principle at work here is that your long-term money sits in your money fund until you decide how to invest it long term. It's also helpful to write down your savings goals:

MY LONG-TERM SAVINGS GOALS

1.
2.
3.
4.
5.

MY SHORT-TERM SAVINGS GOALS

1. Emergencies
2.
3.
4.
5.

Treasury Bonds for Short-Term Savings

If you're interested in absolute "full faith and credit" (of Congress) protection of your principal and perhaps a little better yield, consider intermediate Treasury notes. You can buy them through any broker, Federal Reserve Bank branch, or directly through the Treasury Direct program. Other than the fact that your principal is completely guaranteed if you hold the bonds to maturity, the interest from the bonds is directly deposited into an account of your choice, preferably a money fund.

The newest generation of Treasury Bonds are called I-bonds. The "I" is for inflation and your interest is indexed to the government's Consumer Price Index. If inflation heads up, you get a little better return. These bonds are good places for holding money under ten years—but only for savings goals that require all the money to be there. This applies to savings for college or home down payments.

You can then sign up to open a Treasury Direct account, the Treasury's paperless system of selling and registering bills, notes, and bonds. You'll need to provide your Social Security number, address, and phone. Once you have the basic information entered, you tell the government which account you want your interest (from your

TREASURY DIRECT DETAILS

You can buy Treasury bills, notes, and bonds in minimum "face" amounts of at least $1,000 each. The maturities of the bonds range from 13 weeks to 30 years, although you'll want to stay with bonds with maturities of five years and under.

To open up your account with the U.S. Treasury Department, which will allow you to buy many of their fine products, start with a phone call or a visit to their Web site:

800-943-6864 or 304-480-7955
www.treasurydirect.gov/sec/sectdes.htm

bonds) deposited, usually a savings, checking, or money market account number.

If you want to purchase Treasury bills, you have a choice of 13-week or 26-week bills. The time period refers to their "maturity," or the time at which you get all of your money back plus interest. You can, of course, have all of your money reinvested automatically in new bills. Treasury bills are the most basic savings instruments, as they reflect, or "track" short-term interest rates, which are typically the lowest and safest rates available. In the bond world, the shorter the maturity, the less likely the principal will fluctuate in the open market. But note that with U.S. Treasury securities, if you hold them to maturity and don't sell them, your principal is guaranteed by the full faith and credit of Congress.

The more recently issued I-bonds come in denominations from $50 to $5,000 each and go up to thirty years in maturity. They pay you a fixed rate based on the prevailing interest rates plus a variable rate based on the semiannual Consumer Price Index, which is calculated by the U.S. Department of Labor. So you get a little bonus with I-bonds if inflation shoots up. Interest on I-bonds is compounded semiannually. You can buy up to $30,000 in I-bonds every year. For the purposes of short-term savings, you'd be better off with a combination of I-bonds, Treasury bills, or a money market fund. You really don't need all three, however. If you want to get a better yield at no risk, go with Treasury securities. Most financial institutions can sell you any Treasury security. Brokers also sell them, but will charge you a commission unless you are an extremely good customer.

Money market funds will serve most people's short-term savings needs and are considerably easier to set up and fund. Since they track short-term interest rates, they also track the short-term bond market. If you want to lock in an interest rate for a period of time, go with the Treasury bills or notes. The other difference between money market funds and Treasury products is that your principal is 100% guaranteed with Treasury products if you hold the bonds to maturity.

You can sidestep the guarantee issue by investing in specialized money funds that only invest in government obligations. While these funds do not guarantee principal either, they are slightly more secure than general purpose money funds.

Social Security as a Savings Vehicle

There are two camps when it comes to this controversial subject. The old guard maintains that Social Security can be fixed, it will be there in fifty years and it will be a social insurance safety net for the next two generations. The new guard is much more pessimistic and asserts that unless the system is taken apart, privatized like a mutual fund, and handed back to people like a 401(k)-type account, it will certainly go bust in 2030. The truth lies somewhere in between.

First of all, you can regard Social Security as a safety net because only a political cataclysm will make it into a private stock mutual fund. As social insurance, it's meant to supplement retirement income and not be the sole means of support for anyone—even though for about one-third of Social Security recipients today, that's exactly what it is. It isn't a savings vehicle because you can't control the yield, you have no access to the money until you reach retirement age, and you can't decide how the money is invested. It was meant to relieve poverty in old age. It's not a pension plan.

What Social Security really is, is more akin to fire insurance. If something drastic happens, you will get money to rebuild your house or buy another one. If you don't have any money for retirement, Social Security will back you up, but like fire insurance, it isn't designed to produce wealth. Social Security also provides a death benefit for the family of a wage earner, a disability benefit if you are permanently disabled, and a small burial benefit. If offered as a private insurance plan, the premiums for Social Security would be exorbitant and you wouldn't buy it. That's because insurers and mutual fund companies would take a high percentage of your money in the way of expenses for administration, management, sales, and other items that Social Security does for very little.

Why Social Security Will Endure: We'll Need It

So, if Social Security isn't a savings plan, why should we regard it as one? In the first place, Social Security retirement benefits are indexed to inflation. When you need the money, it will at least *keep pace* with inflation. The money's also guaranteed by Congress. Money you invest in the stock market is not. At worst, Social Security is like a pokey certificate of deposit that pays you a paltry supplement if you have no other retirement money. At best, it's a little bonus if you have saved for retirement.

What happens to Social Security in the future will, as I write this, be an interesting chapter in American history. Although a small portion of it *may* be privatized to allow investment in the stock market, I predict that the system will be bolstered. People will be added to the system (e.g., making government employees contribute to it) and perhaps raising the retirement age (to receive Social Security benefits), which is what a special commission headed by Alan Greenspan did in 1983. Congress will be forced to maintain the guaranteed benefits and the inflation indexing because stocks do not provide guarantees and it would be political suicide to tie in this massive safety net to a market that could collapse when people are ready to retire. More important, once baby boomers and their parents join forces to support it—because it is the best sure-thing deal of any government program—it will not only be strengthened, it will be expanded. And there will also be reforms of private plans like IRAs and 401(k)s to allow even more flexibility in terms of contributions and withdrawals.

Now back to why Social Security should be regarded as a virtual savings plan. If you can't withdraw your contributions to Social Security until retirement age, what good is it as a savings vehicle? Answer: Because it's there and it accumulates over your working life. The more you earn (actually an average of lifetime earnings) and the longer you work, the larger the benefit. Your retirement benefit is so simple to figure out, all you need to do is request the Social Security Administration statement form either online (www. ssa.gov) or by telephone (800-772-1213). Here's what the statement tells you:

- How much income, reported over your working life, is taxed for Social Security. This won't include cash payments, only salary from which FICA taxes were deducted.
- How much your retirement benefit will be at your retirement age—from 65 to 67 depending on when you were born (see table below).
- How much your retirement benefit will be reduced if you take Social Security at age 62.

Once you get your statement, you can see how much is due you when you retire, how much of a disability benefit would be gained if you are permanently impaired (unable to work), and the death benefit paid to your survivors. Unless Congress totally dismembers the system or fails to fund it, this is your money. You can count on it, and although the mechanism by which it gets to you is a little fuzzy, count it as *virtual* savings.

When you get your statement in the mail, it tells you two things: how much you've "saved" and how much you'll get in terms of benefits. I'll show you my statement to give you an example:

Retirement at age 62, your payment
will be about $894 a month
   [Everybody qualifies for Social Security
at 62, but your benefit is reduced until you
reach full retirement age]
   If you continue working until
your full retirement age [66 and 6 months
for me since I was born in 1957], your
payment would be about $1,233 a month
   At age 70 [they give you a little bonus] $1,587 a month
Disability [if you can't work] $1,583 a month
Family [if you die, your
survivors get a maximum] $2,840 a month
   Your child $1,217 a month

Your spouse [caring for a child]	$1,217 a month
Your spouse who reaches full retirement age	$1,623 a month
Death Benefit [one-time payment for spouse or minor]	$255
Estimated Taxes paid for Society Security:	
You paid	$50,278
Your employers paid	$50,576
Estimated Taxes paid for Medicare	
You paid	$12,025
Your employers paid	$12,025

What do I conclude after reading my statement, and what can you conclude after reading yours? First, Social Security is a good deal. It combines a retirement annuity, a disability plan, and survivorship benefit into one payroll tax. You won't be able to find all three of these products under one policy anywhere for what you pay the Social Security Administration.

The second conclusion is that I won't be able to live on Social Security, so I need to save more to maintain my standard of living in my seventh decade and beyond. This is a safe assumption for most of us. No matter what happens to Social Security, we will need to start saving for short- and long-term goals. So read your statement and start saving.

The government—through conservative management of our payroll contributions—will only do so much. True, some changes will be made to Social Security to stave off the projected shortfall in the SSA trust fund (the big savings account for Social Security), which is estimated to go into the red in 2037 when most baby boomers are retired. I wouldn't count on Washington to provide a solution that will provide the savings you need to live comfortably into your ninth and tenth decades. I also wouldn't waste much time worrying about whether or not it will be there when you retire. It *will* be there in some form. It's the most successful government program in the history of the country and voters know that and will protect it.

What you need is an automatic way of growing money that will make you less reliant upon Social Security, which is what I'll be discussing in subsequent chapters. You already have the means to an end with a money market fund or Treasury bonds. Now you can tap some of your inner resources, or take the advice of writer Edward Abbey: "You long for success? Start at the bottom; dig down."

You'll also need to fully fund tax-deferred plans of your own. If you don't have any now, you can set them up yourself with little fuss. If you currently have a company-sponsored plan, fully fund it and set up as many supplemental tax-deferred vehicles as you can. If you are pensionless, sally forth to the next chapter.

SUMMARY: YOUR SAVINGS VEHICLES

1. After you've identified where you can save money, and how much, save it.
2. Choose a money market account or fund that pays competitive yields with minimal or no fees.
3. Fund your money funds through automatic debits or other sources.
4. Identify your long- and short-term savings goals.
5. Use Treasury bonds for guaranteed short-term savings goals.
6. Obtain your statement from the Social Security Administration and review it.
7. Start funding your savings and investment plans.
8. Start researching investments that will he funded (see next chapter).

CHAPTER 5

Creating Your Own Kitchen-Table Pension Plan

To be rich, regardless of his fortune or lack of it, a man must live by his own values. If those values are not personally meaningful, then no amount of money gained can hide the emptiness of a life without them.

—J. Paul Getty

It's ironic that when it comes to investing from scratch, I really don't have to go much further than my own family, in this case my wife, my father-, mother-, and brother-in-law. They embody why people come to America. Belfast in the early '80s was a festering wound of a city. The police and British troops were targets of IRA bombs. Any public place would be bombed for any reason by any of a whole host of nationalist and republican groups, each justifying their murders for some cause buried in the politics of some other century.

Kathleen's mother, Mary Theresa, was in a building when it was blown up. She survived, but only with the help of tranquilizers. Kathleen was taunted on a regular basis and was threatened when she walked down the wrong street. Her brother Martin's severe asthma was aggravated by tear gas, so he went to boarding school in England. Being a Catholic in Northern Ireland was like being an African American in the South before 1970. You were a constant target.

When the Conlons arrived in America in 1981, Kathleen gave up a college scholarship. She could have gone to college free of charge, but instead came over with her family. Her father left reluctantly. Both Joe and Martin had been driving cabs on the treacherous lanes of Falls Road, a serpentine street through Catholic West Belfast. Stephen, the youngest, they all felt, would be sucked into the vortex of sectarian politics.

The first few years in America were rough for the Conlons. They all worked: Theresa in a sweat shop of a drapery factory, Joe in a printing ink plant, Martin in a hot printing plant, and Kathleen in a restaurant, a job she rode her bike to, even though it was several miles away. The transition was awkward and difficult in their tiny, rented house. They gradually all made more money, however; Stephen went to college and Theresa was able to start her own window-treatment shop.

Like many emigrant tales, this story in progress is going well. Despite having to retire due to a disability, Joe and Theresa paid off their townhouse and bought a new one, Kathleen started her own profitable business, Martin joined Theresa's business, and Stephen took over a business from his father-in-law. All of the Conlons emerged from poverty to find a New Prosperity.

The linchpin to all of this was well-funded retirement plans. Joe fully funded his company plans and IRAs. Kathleen set up a SEP-IRA for her business to cover her and her brother Stephen, who worked for her a few years. Now Stephen continues to fund his plan and Martin is fully funding his. Everyone except Stephen is a

SAVINGS OVER TIME

Time	You save	Interest	Total
10 yrs.	$6,000	$3,676	$9,676
20 yrs.	$12,000	$21,394	$33,394
30 yrs.	$18,000	$73,537	$91,537

member of the Wall Street Prowlers investment club, which you'll be reading more about.

The Golden Age of Retirement Vehicles

Welcome to the golden age of retirement vehicles. No matter where you are financially—or where you are from—there's a vehicle that will allow you to build tax-deferred growth. Are you self-employed? You can set up your own plan. Partially employed? No problem, there's a range of plans for you. Even if you are working in the non-profit sector, there are plenty of options.

It wasn't always a golden age for retirement plans. When I entered the workforce in the mid-1970s it was the dark age, unless you worked for a large corporation. There was no such thing as a "defined-contribution" plan for most employees. Companies didn't hire mutual fund firms to manage employee plans. The company you worked for either offered a pension plan in the form of a defined-benefit plan—for which you had to work fifteen to twenty years to qualify (vesting)—or you were on your own. My first three employers had no pension plan at all. It wasn't until I worked for a company partially owned by a telephone company that I got an employer-sponsored vehicle to contribute to—and that was in the mid-1980s. At the time, if you bounced from employer to employer in search of better wages (my first job as a cub reporter for a community newspaper paid me $9,600 a year), you had nothing unless you saved on your own, which I did.

There have been more "self-directed" tax-deferred plans set up in the last fifteen years in the United States (and other Western countries) than in all of recorded history. This is not an idle boast. You can now set up a variety of plans, don't need to tie them into a single employer, and can invest in more than 6,000 mutual funds and countless stocks. Most of this revolution came about when Congress realized that employers were by and large not taking care of their workers' retirements. Of course, if you worked for companies like IBM, GE, GM, or Procter & Gamble, these big companies generally took care of you—or got rid of you—by cutting "early retirement" checks to older workers they wanted to trim from their payrolls. Unfortunately, small businesses with under 250 employees employ the vast majority of Americans and it's rare for them to be offered 401(k) plans.

Enter the defined-contribution plan, which took a lot of the burden off employers, so more employers were able to offer them. An obscure section of the U.S. tax code had made them possible for years, but it wasn't until Ted Benna, the inventor of the modern 401(k)-type plan, found out how to make them work for employers on a large scale that they became popular. The now-famous 401(k) and 403(b) plans and their many counterparts fueled the revolution. They were inexpensive to administer because they allowed a third party like an insurer, brokerage, or mutual fund manager to become the administrator and portfolio manager instead of the employer. This not only lowered the costs of providing the plans, it opened up the plan to better management and more options for employees. Under the old defined-benefit model, there was one, huge institutional portfolio managed for the entire company or, in the case of some union-sponsored plans, for an entire group of industries. These pension-management schemes not only produced mediocre returns, but they were highly regulated, sometimes pilfered, and expensive to run. Employees had absolutely no control over how the pension funds were invested, were required to be "vested" by working for an employer for decades, and couldn't take their pension to another employer.

The most flexible part of the new defined-contribution plans were that they shifted the responsibility of managing money to the individual worker, who could not only choose managers but different fund objectives and move their money around to suit their risk tolerance. Seemingly overnight, workers could choose between stock index, aggressive growth, overseas, bonds, and money market funds and allocate accordingly. Workers essentially became their own portfolio managers, free to move in and out of the stock and bond markets at will, making their own decisions on the best funds for their place in life. And that's where we're at today, only the picture is getting better with each passing year.

The Political Impetus for Better Retirement Plans

Congress is facing the ultimate demographic reality of this nation's largest generation—the 77 million baby boomers looking at age sixty-five in 2011. Although not all of the leading-edge boomers will quit the workforce then and take Social Security, those born between 1946 and 1964 will want maximum flexibility in their tax-deferred plans—even more than what's offered today. This means plans that will allow you to contribute more and withdraw without penalties, and will provide tax-based incentives to do so. It *will* happen. It's only a matter of time when baby boomers become even more politically active and get representatives elected who can legislate for their unique financial needs. In the meantime, what's available is more than enough to get you started. Taking advantage of them is a fairly streamlined sorting process. The first order of business, however, is taking advantage of what's available now through your employer.

At Work: Fully Fund All Pretax Plans

Don't hesitate. When you sign up for paycheck withdrawal into your company's defined-contribution plan, not only is the money going right into your tax-deferred plan but the only taxes taken out are for Social Security and Medicare. No federal or state taxes are withheld.

Keep in mind that these plans work best when you fully fund them, preferably with *pretax* money. That way, you're getting tax-deferred growth in any number of ways. You're getting up to a third of your money returned to you without having to do much of anything—just set it aside automatically every month.

As a rule, fund all of your pretax plans first. Then move into plans that are funded with post-tax contributions. If you have a 401(k), 403(b), or SIMPLE, fully fund them before putting money into IRAs, Roths, and SEP-IRAs; these plans are funded with *post-tax* dollars.

If your employer matches the funds you contribute, that's "free money." If your employer matches 1% on a minimum 3% contribution, one out of three dollars are found money that you don't have to contribute. Your return on the employer match: 100%! The more generous the match, the more you should participate. If you don't think you can afford the reduction in salary, just consider this: if you don't get the money in your pay envelope, you can't spend it because it's being saved automatically. You get a break on your income taxes, because your taxable liability drops by the amount of your contributions. It could mean the difference between a higher and lower tax bracket.

I know the folly of contributing less to my 401(k) in hopes of grabbing more take-home pay. I cut my contribution in half and paid more in income taxes. After my employer withheld federal and state taxes, my take-home pay was only tens of dollars more. It wasn't worth it. You can ask your employer how much money you'll actually receive after taxes. It's a paltry amount. So why give the money to the government if you don't have to?

How Much Money Will Be in Your Tax-Deferred Plan?

When I teach classes on investing, this is my favorite part for math-challenged folks like me. To get a simple prediction of how much your money will be worth over time all you need is the amount (of the principal) and the rate of return. Then, you use what is called a Rule of 72, or the rate at which money doubles. All you have do is divide the rate of return by 72. If you don't want to do the math (few do), here are some benchmarks:

Rate of Return	Time in Which Your Money Doubles
4%	18 years (average whole-life insurance %)
5%	14.4 years (savings account yield)
6%	12 years (money market fund)
7%	10.3 years (intermediate-term bond)
8%	9 years (paltry stock mutual fund)
9%	8 years (mediocre stock mutual fund)
10%	7.2 years (somewhat better stock fund)

Rate of Return	Time in Which Your Money Doubles
11%	6.5 years (average growth-stock fund return)
12%	6 years (small-stock growth fund)
15%	4.8 years (growth stocks)

Choosing the Right Plan on Your Own

The following plans are the most commonly offered vehicles by employers.

401(k) Plans

Who qualifies: Any employee who is vested, which is usually a period of a few months or a year. The employer determines the vesting period, but it's generally a year or less for most defined-contribution plans like 401(k)s.

Contributions: Up to 11% of your annual pretax income.

Benefits: The single best vehicle today to build wealth over time. Once you're vested, the money is yours. You can "roll it over" into another qualified plan (such as a rollover IRA) when you leave your employer. Typically, you'll have a choice of mutual funds, monitoring, retirement planning calculators, and loan provisions.

Restrictions: Unless you are incapacitated, need the money for "qualified" higher-education expenses (tuition but not room and board), or a first-home purchase, you face a 10% penalty plus income taxes at your marginal rate if you withdraw funds before age 59½. You can, however, take a 72(t) exemption before age 59½ under the IRS code, but you are locking in monthly payments based on your life expectancy. You'll need an accountant or financial planner to set that up, as the math gets complicated. (See my *Retire Early—and Live the Life You Want Now,* Henry Holt, 2000, for more details if you are in the position to retire early).

Named after a once obscure section of the U.S. tax code, the 401(k) combines pretax payroll withdrawals with separate mutual funds. You tell your company to deduct a specified amount per paycheck and the funds are deposited into mutual funds that are independently managed. The pretax funds reduce your taxable income and are invested on a tax-deferred basis. The funds are also all yours. You can withdraw the money (see restrictions above), get loans from your plan, and transfer—or "roll over"—the funds into another fund or tax-deferred account when you leave the company or retire. Most companies will match your contribution dollar for dollar up to the first 8% of your salary. If you earn $30,000 a year and your company matches 5%, you end up saving $3,000 per year. So you get 100% return on *your* contribution before it's even invested in the mutual funds. Like IRAs, you are penalized (10% surtax plus income tax) if you withdraw funds before age 59½ unless you can prove a hardship (severe illness, education expenses). Although nonprofits generally offer 403(b) plans (see below), 401(k)s can also be offered by tax-exempt organizations. Variations on 401(k) or defined-contribution plans that defer your earnings and invest pretax dollars include thrift plans and company stock plans or employee stock ownership plans. Again, these packages allow you to save pretax dollars, reduce your taxable income and almost always include a matching amount from your company. This is the first stop on the New Prosperity train.

403(b)s, 457s

These plans are essentially the same as a 401(k) but are available only to nonprofit institutions. The 457 is largely for state employees and is technically a deferred compensation plan. Schools, universities, hospitals, charitable groups, and other nonprofits offer these plans to their employees.

The rules are similar to 401(k)s and you may even have a greater choice of plan options and funds.

Plans You Can Start Yourself

SEP-IRAs

A simple pension plan to set up for yourself if you have a company of your own, the SEP-IRA requires a simple four-page application. Even small companies can offer these plans to their employees with a minimum amount of paperwork and offer several mutual funds.

Who qualifies: Any regular employee of a small company or self-employed individual.

Contributions: Up to 15% or annual salary, capped at $24,000.

Benefits: The paperwork consists of only a few pages. You can also invest in other IRAs if you have a SEP. Employers can make pretax contributions.

Restrictions: The SEP is less flexible than a Keogh (see below). If one is offered, it must be offered to all full-time employees and is funded only through employer contributions. Also subject to the "59½" penalty and related rules (like all other forms of IRAs).

SIMPLE IRAs

A more advanced pretax plan for small companies, the SIMPLE is a more recent innovation that provides 401(k)-type features like payroll deductions with slightly more paperwork than the SEP. It replaced the SAR-SEP as of January 1, 1997.

Who qualifies: Any employee in a firm under 100 employees.

Contributions: Up to $6,000 a year. Employer can match up to 3% of total compensation up to a maximum $3,200.

Benefits: It's an uncomplicated pretax plan, which any small company can set up. The employer match makes it an even better deal, much like a 401(k).

Restrictions: There's more administration, but it may be a good choice for companies employing 100 employees or less. Unlike the 401(k), the SIMPLE doesn't have stringent requirements that all employees must be offered the plan and there's no "discrimination/top-heavy" testing that must be done with 401(k)s. The cap is $6,000, so you may do better with a Keogh.

Keoghs

The oldest pretax vehicle for small companies, Keoghs allow for several types of employee contributions, but require a lot of paperwork. Generally they are not used as much anymore because the SIMPLE and SEP plans are easier to start and administer.

Who qualifies: Employees or partners with self-employment income, including proprietors who file Schedule C or partners filing Schedule E.

Contributions: Up to $30,000 a year or 13.04% of self-employment income for profit-sharing plans (see below) or $30,000 or 20% of income for a money-purchase plan.

Benefits: It's a solid vehicle for most small businesses with a high contribution limit. You can also invest in a conventional IRA if you have a Keogh.

Restrictions: You have a choice between a "money purchase" or "profit sharing" plan. The former is a mandatory fixed-percentage contribution by the employer; the latter is more flexible, based on yearly profits.

Conventional IRAs

Also called "traditional" IRAs, these accounts allow you to contribute $2,000 and deduct it (if you qualify). You'll be looking at deductible or nondeductible versions, depending on your household income. Even if you can't deduct it, set one up anyway. Your money is still growing tax-deferred.

Who qualifies: You can qualify if you make less than $150,000 a year for married couples filing jointly and $32,000 for singles and heads of household.

Contributions: $2,000 if the taxpayer is not participating in an employer plan. Otherwise, see restrictions below.

Benefits: You can deduct $2,000 per spouse if you qualify and enjoy tax-deferred growth or income. The IRA for your spouse is cleverly called a "spousal IRA."

Restrictions: The $150,000 limit applies if only one spouse has a qualified retirement plan at work; otherwise the limit is $160,000 for joint filers and $42,000 for singles and heads of household. If both spouses have company retirement plans, then the limit is $62,000 for joint filers. You can open up this account or a Roth IRA, but not both. You also are forced to withdraw the money when you reach 70½.

Roth IRAs

Although contributions to a Roth are not tax deductible, you can make withdrawals without penalty if you invest the money for at least five years.

KITCHEN-TABLE TIP

INDEX FUNDS FOR YOUR TAX-DEFERRED PLANS

For maximum performance at low cost for your tax-deferred plans, choose a stock index mutual fund, which is a breadbasket of stocks that are never traded. These funds are offered by all major mutual fund groups and are perfect for IRAs and company plans. An all-market index fund earned 15.8% over the past fifteen years, beating the average stock mutual fund by 4.6 percentage points per year.

Who qualifies: If you make less than $160,000 (married/joint filers) or $110,000 if you are single or head of household filers.

Contributions: You're limited to $2,000 (per person) per year or your total compensation for the year. The way the IRS phrases it is "the lesser of your earned income or $2,000." In plain English, you max out at $2,000.

Benefits: You can also pull money out tax-free to buy a home or pay for education expenses as long as you hold the money for at least five years. This vehicle is a worthwhile supplement to other plans. Always fully fund your pretax or deductible plans first, but this plan is a must-have if you qualify and have funded every other plan. Even if you are near retirement, this is a good deal because, unlike a conventional IRA, you are not forced to withdraw it at age 70½.

Self-Directed IRAs

These IRAs are essentially accounts you establish with a financial-services provider such as a brokerage house, mutual fund firm, bank, or insurer. There are also mega-financial companies that embrace all of these services—Citicorp-Travelers, GE, Fidelity, Vanguard, Prudential, et al.—and offer them as well.

A self-directed IRA is best for someone looking for maximum flexibility. If you want to hold individual stocks or bonds, this is the only one that will permit it. The same withdrawal rules apply as to conventional IRAs (no penalty-free withdrawals before age 59½). You can even hold stocks within dividend-reinvestment plans, but that gets to be a little tricky, and only a handful of companies will handle the paperwork for that.

10 THINGS TO AVOID IN A COMPANY PLAN

1. Don't put all of your belongings in one boat. Never invest all of your money in one stock (especially company stock), mutual fund, bond, or guaranteed investment account (avoid at all costs). You need growth among diversified funds.

2. Diversify simply. All you really need is a growth stock index fund, an international fund, and an aggressive growth fund that invests in health care, technology, and telecommunications (in other words, high-growth industries). The most basic all-purpose allocation is 33% in stock index funds, 33% in international funds, and 33% in aggressive growth or small-company funds (see chapter 7 for more details).

3. Forget about bonds. This is a huge mistake in a tax-deferred plan. You want to grow your principal, not your income. And putting your money in bonds isn't the "safer" alternative, either. The bond market can lose up to one-third in any given year if interest rates are rising. Your best long-term return is in stocks over a decade or more.

4. Stay put. Most plan managers allow you the ability to switch from fund to fund through telephone services and the Internet. Take a close look at your allocations once a year in January and switch out of your losers.

5. Look at fees. All similar index funds have one important difference: their fees or expense ratios. The lower the expense ratio, the higher the return in index funds. It's pretty simple, but they're all the same. Don't pay any up-front sales charges or "contingent" fees through a broker or bank. The fees will reduce your return for no greater service.

6. Look for account providers who waive IRA custodial fees. These deals are offered all the time. You save from $10 to $25 per account. Even if your fund company won't waive the fees, don't forget to deduct them on your income tax if you itemize.

7. Do the paperwork yourself. Most IRA setup applications are one or two pages. If you do it yourself, you'll have a much better understanding of the restrictions and funding requirements. If you run into trouble, nearly every account provider has a toll-free number to call. You don't need a broker or banker to do this for you.

8. Open as many accounts as you can. If you fund a Roth in addition to your company plan (and your gross adjusted income is less than $150,000 for joint filers), go for it. It's all compounding tax-deferred and that's what you want. The more the merrier.

9. Keep and review all statements. Keep statements in a folder. See how they are doing once a year, although you'll get one per account every quarter. Also keep in mind you can deduct the custodial fees if you itemize on your taxes.

10. Keep contributing. It's so easy to forget about that Roth or conventional IRA once you set it up. If the $2,000 is too much at one time, break it up into smaller portions; that's $166.66 a month.

SUMMARY

1. Take the time to research all the different types of retirement plans.
2. If your employer offers a plan, research it and fully fund it.
3. If you are self-employed or want to supplement your employer plan, set up the plan appropriate to your needs (SEP, SIMPLE, Roth). Fund those plans after you've funded all of your pretax plans.
4. Fund your plans for maximum growth. Choose aggressive growth, index, and international funds for basic allocation.
5. Review your funds' performances every year and make adjustments to dump losers. Keep all statements on file.

CHAPTER 6

Long-Haulers:
Stocks to Buy and Hold

Every man is a consumer, and ought to be a producer. He fails to make his place good in the world, unless he not only pays his debt, but also adds something to the common wealth.
—Ralph Waldo Emerson, *Wealth*

The world is no longer contained by our direct experience. We can be connected to so many others without seeing or touching them. We can be linked to people on the other side of the earth without actually seeing them or hearing their voice. This anti-sensual globalism is reshaping the way we communicate in profound ways. In that context, I suppose I should not be awed at Gary Meier's project. His WINvest investment club never really meets. It's a cyberclub on the Internet.

The principle of WINvest is simple. They solicit members from the Internet and buy stocks. There are no required monthly investments to make, no meetings to attend. There's nothing to show up for and you don't need to worry about somebody stealing your credit card number. It's a concept that exists out there in cyberspace, but serves the same role as other investment clubs.

Started by Gary and his son-in-law in Indianapolis, WINvest has members from coast to coast. You can apply on the Web site and join for $25. If you don't like what you see, your money is refundable in 30 days. The newsletters, stock lists, and analyses are all posted on the Web site.

"We're kind of strange," Meier says whimsically. "We elect managing partners biannually. Each new member recommends a stock and agrees to watch one. We buy all of our stocks through dividend reinvestment plans [DRPs]."

How is the electronic mode of investing working if partners can't shout at each other over their favorite stock picks? WINvest owns pharmaceutical companies such as Abbott Labs (the largest holding), Eli Lilly, and Pharmacia. Meier admits the club's picks have been on the conservative side in avoiding technology stocks, but they are profitable. He estimates their annual return has been around 20% since they started in 1996, not a market beater, but certainly respectable.

As in nearly every club, several generations are involved. A grandmother who is a member has funded two grandchildren's member-

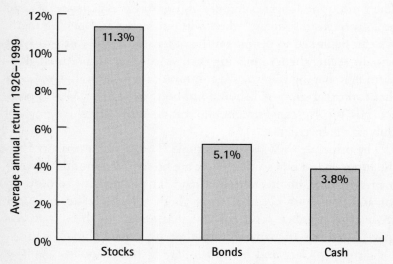

STOCKS PERFORM OVERTIME

Stocks have outperformed bonds and short-term Treasury bills (cash) over the long term.

ships; one cashed out when he was eighteen. Meier, who is an insurance company project manager, has involved his daughter and son-in-law. Everyone who is a member picks up ideas for their own accounts.

Meier says the cyberclub approach, though lacking the human touch, avoids some common problems clubs have with certain members dominating the proceedings.

"I was a member of a [conventional] investment club and the meetings were boring events. There would be office politics and 'bulldozers' pontificating at the meetings. I withdrew after a year."

While WINvest is far from a typical club, it embodies some classic club traits, such as:

- Centers the discussions on quality stocks to buy and at what prices.
- Doesn't force members to make investment decisions if they are not ready.
- Focuses on dividends and reinvesting those dividends with their 34 holdings.
- When companies merge or consolidate, they are replaced with new ones.
- In personal portfolios such as Gary's, stocks are mixed with mutual funds for greater diversification.
- Each member can invest a set amount per month, but they benefit the most if they do research and monitoring of stocks.

Beginning to Buy Stocks

Whether you get your stock ideas on the Internet or in a club of your own, you need to start with some ideas. Saving wasn't such a difficult process once you put your money market fund on auto-pilot, set up your company funds, and started channeling money away from spending, was it? Now that you have a battery for your growth vehicle, you need an engine. That's where stocks and mutual funds come in. This chapter will deal with the simple rules on picking stocks for the long term. It's considerably simpler than doing your taxes. I can pick stocks, but I leave taxes to my tax consultant.

It may surprise you, but there are only five basic rules that are the bedrock of investment club principles as laid out by the National Association of Investors Corporation. They have been working for years, even though only a handful of Internet stocks defy these rules from time to time. This "fundamental analysis" school of investing says that "earnings drive growth." That means when earnings rise, the stock price usually rises. Although this doesn't always happen because the market isn't as efficient as some economists say it is, most of the time you will make money if earnings are on the ascent.

When investors see a company growing, its value increases because they are willing to pay more for it—and bid up prices in the market. Ever notice when a hot car comes on the market and people line up to buy it? If you try to ask for a discount on the sticker price, the dealer will have a good chuckle. Buyers are then willing to pay premiums. Growth and desirability create demand and spur prices. Stocks are no different, although, unlike a car, growth stocks will appreciate, pay dividends, and build capital. Cars just rust, need lots of maintenance, and decline in value.

Long term, it's difficult to lose money on your entire portfolio if you've done your homework first. Some of your stocks will turn out to be total dogs. A handful will be consistent. Some will be stunning. Hold on to your winners and know what makes for a loser you need to sell. If you are in a club or by yourself, the following guidelines boil down the process.

FIVE FUNDAMENTAL RULES OF STOCK-PICKING

1. Find quality companies that are growing earnings consistently from 10% to 15% per year. A stock value will double in five years at 15% per year growth rate.
2. Earnings over the past five years are some indication of how you can predict future growth. Sales and earnings per share should be increasing in lockstep with earnings. Look for companies with at least five years of earnings.

3 Buy a stock for the long term. Try to look five or ten years down the road. Where is management headed? Is there a solid future for this company?

4. Keep your costs low and your commitment high. Get into dividend-reinvestment or direct-investment plans and cut out the broker. Reinvest all dividends.

5. Keep investing and monitoring by automatically purchasing shares on a regular basis to reduce market risk. If earnings don't grow, monitor for a year and see if a turnaround is imminent.

Finding Stocks to Buy

The first thing teachers tell you in creative writing class is "write about something you know." The same is true with investing. The legendary investor Peter Lynch tells beginning investors to start with the shopping mall. What are the hot retailers? Why do people shop there? Perhaps you are familiar with a specific industry (the one you're in now) or buy certain products or services. When it comes to stock-picking, you'll have better insights into companies if you know what they make or do and can explain their business to others. The following are some places to begin when looking for companies to invest in:

- **Local Employers.** Major employers close to home are good places to start. You can talk to people who work for the company and own the stock. Chances are, if they are long-term employees—and they've held their company's stock—they can tell you how well (or poorly) they've done. I live down the street from a Motorola plant and the company's headquarters is about 15 miles away (more on Motorola as an example later in this chapter).

- **Local Retailers.** Any commercial district of any urban area will feature the largest retailers of nearly everything. For starters, there's McDonald's, Wendy's, Home Depot, Wal-Mart, Starbucks, The Gap, and Dunkin' Donuts. If there's a national chain, there's a good probability there's a stock behind it. If you know what a company sells, it makes a lot of the more intensive analysis easier.

- **Business-to-Business Suppliers.** You know which companies your employer deals with and how they perform. It's no secret that the best business-to-business companies have been around for a long time and continue to grow because they are well managed. This is true in any business and scouting these stocks is based on consistent management, which you may be in unique position to evaluate.

- **Major Regional Industries.** You may live in a region that's dominated by one or a handful of major industries. In Pittsburgh, there are few people over fifty who don't know something about the steel industry (past and present). If you live in the Silicon Valley area, high technology is the big player. In New York, it's Wall Street firms or big banks. In Houston, it's oil and gas. Regional investing is a great way to start because you are again building upon what you and your local club members may already know.

- **Things You Buy and Keep.** Families often stick to certain brands of vehicles, food, clothing, and "durable goods," such as major appliances. As an editor for *Consumers Digest,* I've had a unique overview of what makes or breaks a consumer goods company. It's no surprise that quality manufacturers tend to grow profits and stay in business longer than shoddy ones.

Now you have some idea where to start. Once you have a short list of companies to investigate, meet with your club or throw them in a pile for future study. Then it's off to the library for some preliminary research. Two immediate questions will need to be answered:

1. Is it a public company? Does it sell its stock to the public? Say you like the maker of Pledge and Raid, which is made by S.C. Johnson & Son of Racine, Wisconsin. Though it's a solid company that's been profitable for a long time, it's a *privately held* company. You can't buy the stock unless you're an employee or a member of the Johnson family. So focus on companies that have a stock that's traded on the major stock exchanges (NYSE, AMEX, NASDAQ).

2. Is the company profitable? Okay, sure, a lot of people have made billions on Internet start-ups that haven't made a dime. The plain fact is that most of them will be out of business or sold within the next five years. It's a basic rule of capitalism that at least 80% of all new businesses fail in the first years of operation. So concentrate on companies that have at least five years of earnings. If a company has no profits, it won't grow its stock price. I know there are lots of exceptions, but let's focus on companies with proven track records.

KITCHEN-TABLE TIP

CAN YOU DO BETTER WITH BONDS?

In investing, it's what you keep that counts. Inflation, taxes, and administrative/brokerage fees reduce your total or *real* return. So what's better over time? Stocks or bonds? Here's the historical record of why stocks are best over the long run:

	Historical Record Returns 1926–1999	Estimated Returns 2000–2030
Bonds	6%	5%
Bonds—after inflation	3%	3%
Stocks	11%	8%
Stocks—after inflation	8%	6%

This model assumes past inflation of 3% per year and a future rate of 2%. Historical record covers the period 1926 to 1999. After inflation, your best financial investment is still stocks, preferably invested in a tax-deferred account.

Source: Ibbotson Associates.

How to Read *Value Line*

Once your companies have passed those first two tests, it's time to hit the books. The first tool to grab is *The Value Line Investment Survey,* which is either behind the reference desk or shelved with other business reference materials in your public library. *Value Line* is a big black binder of individual stock reports grouped by industry. It has a master index that will tell you what page your stock is listed on. Then grab the big binder and copy the report, which is one page of numbers and a graph.

Table of Summary and Index Contents. This is where you begin your *Value Line* journey. You can pick stocks by name in the index or by industry. I've always found the industry classifications a bit obsolete since modern corporations are involved in so many different businesses and overlap in their industry headings. For example, some telecommunications companies are also into technology. A company like General Electric makes lightbulbs and credit cards, so it would be difficult to find the company by industry heading. Nevertheless, if you are searching by companies by specific industry groups, they'll be listed in categories ranging from advertising to water utilities. The summary listings of each stock covered will give recent prices (not recent enough) and "timeliness" and "safety" ratings. You'll also find P/Es (price-to-earnings ratios), estimated earnings, estimated dividend yields, and earnings for the most recent quarter.

Timeliness, Performance, and Safety. These two ratings are based on a numeric system; 1 is highest, 4 is below average. *Timeliness* examines whether the stock is a good buy based on the most recent price in their survey. *Safety* tells you about the downside of a stock, that is, how likely the price will decline given all that is known about the company. These two indicators will be indispensable in analyzing your stocks. While they are guideposts, they are hardly the sole factors in determining whether to buy a stock. Other factors worth noting are financial strength (A+ is highest), price stability (5 is highest), earnings predictability, and beta. Performance generally refers to earnings growth. These numbers give you a composite picture of how to predict earnings and volatility. The beta is a number that shows you how the stock did relative to a market index, which is the S&P 500 for most growth stocks. A beta of 1.00 equals the average volatility of the market index, or just plain "market." A beta of 2.00 is twice as volatile as the average stock in the index. While many investors confuse beta with risk, it will tell you how much a stock price jumps around or "deviates" from the average.

Price Graph. This graph will plot high and low market prices over the past nine years and predict the price in the coming year. The prices are charting as a "moving average," sales volume, and "relative strength," which mirrors the price. The graph will also show stock splits. You'll want to use the numbers of the highs and lows to figure average prices.

Financials. The "heart" of the *Value Line* page is chock-full of figures on sales, earnings per share, P/Es, profit, tax rates, and related financial information. You'll need to find sales, net profit, P/Es, and earnings per share to calculate five-year averages.

Commentary. In a tiny box below the graph, in really small type, is the commentary. This looks at major changes within the company, and you have to read it carefully, as it can be subtle. The last sentences usually tell you where the company may be headed. Acquisitions and divestitures are noted here along with a general description of what the company does. There's also basic information about company officers, address, Web site, and phone numbers. You'll need this information to order 10-Ks, annual reports, and related information.

Rates and Averages. On the lower left-hand side of the page, you'll see averages for sales, earnings, dividends by year and quarters. There's also total shareholder return in the lower right and debt and asset information in the center. You're mainly concerned with five-year rates on sales, earnings, and dividends.

What You Need to Do with *Value Line*

Bring the *Value Line* information on the stock(s) you've selected to your club meeting or your own investment session. Present the stock's five-year record and averages on earnings, P/E, sales, and dividends. Make notes on whether *Value Line* recommends the stock, its timeliness and safety. Also check the recent share price (the prior day's closing) and see if *Value Line* is on the mark with their assessment based on the recent closing price. If the price has taken a hit or soared tremendously it may make the stock a better or more costly buy. Then check *Value Line* against other resources and do your own analysis (read on).

Other Useful Resources

Standard & Poor's is similar to *Value Line* and can be found in the same place in the library. It's a good second opinion. The numbers will be the same as *Value Line,* but the prediction of future growth and the rating system will be different.

Morningstar (either online at www.morningstar.com or in the library), which rates stocks in addition to mutual funds, places much more emphasis on its analysis and commentary, and is useful for a third opinion.

Once you've done your homework, assemble your file and bring it to your next meeting or sit yourself down in a quiet room with no distractions and do your analysis.

How to Read an Annual Report/10-K

As a person who makes a living doing investigative reporting, I can tell you that documents are always the first place to start when figuring out a company's "story." Annual reports are the first of many documents you need to review; the company's 10-K is also a must-read. The annual report, which can be ordered directly from the company's investor relations department or their Web site, is the summation of financial results and management statements for the past year. Although there are some forward-looking statements in the annual reports, take them with a grain of salt—they are rarely negative.

Like the annual report, the company's 10-K report is the company's history over the past year, only without the gloss. It's a "just the facts, ma'am" accounting of where the company has been and where it expects to go. This is the document the company is required to file with the U.S. Securities and Exchange Commission, so it tends to be direct and dry. I've always found a few details that appear in depth in the 10-K that don't appear in the annual report, namely pending litigation and a better explanation of marketing pitfalls. In any case, order both documents and read them. This is what you'll need to pay attention to and note when you are evaluating stocks:

Profits. There are a number of ways of stating profits. "Net income" is the most popular way, which is revenue after all operating costs and taxes are subtracted. There's also "pretax" profit, which doesn't subtract taxes, and "earnings before interest, taxes, depreciation, and amortization" (EBITDA), which is generally regarded as the company's cash flow, or how much money is flowing into the company. You'll need to know if earnings increased from last year and by how much. Double-digit earnings growth is desirable, but may reflect a one-time event such as acquisition of another company or seasonal increases in sales. A five-year trend is most valid in looking at profits. Remember, 15% a year in profit *growth* is a good place to start, but look at the average over a half-decade. If earnings aren't growing, then you won't see any upside in the stock price. There are exceptions, as I've noted before, but sooner or later, the market will value a company based on its ability to make money on a consistent basis.

Revenues. Also known as *sales,* this is also important in a five-year frame. Generally, increases in sales mean bigger profits. Although a company can boost its profitability any number of ways without increasing sales, you want to see that the company's different business lines are growing. Look at each line of business by *segment* and see how sales are growing. A segment may be a division or branch of the company that reports sales separately. In General Electric, for example, "lighting" is a separate segment from "NBC Broadcasting." Ideally, you'll want to see every one of a company's segments show improved sales figures, but that doesn't always happen. If there's a decline in a segment, look for the company's explanation of the downturn and when it expects a recovery. If a major segment or several lines of business are faltering, that's a warning sign. Keep in mind that sales also build a company's *market share,* which also should be noted in the reports. Those with dominant market shares are industry leaders.

Price-Earnings Ratio, Earnings/Share. Also known as the P/E Ratio or simply the P/E, this is a highly scrutinized little number that changes every day. It's the stock price divided by the *earnings per share* (profit divided by number of shares outstanding). P/Es can tell you whether a stock is a bargain or inflated in price. Always compare P/Es of a single company with that of the industry average P/E (you can do this with *Value Line*). A P/E is always a relative yardstick for whether the price is high or low relative to the industry or the company's historical P/E (going back five years). So a low P/E relative to the industry and the company's average P/E is probably a better buy than a high P/E. Of course, the value of the P/E is hotly debated among stock analysts. So look at the P/E in concert with profits and sales. A high P/E is not necessarily a bad omen in and of itself, but it's always desirable to buy at a lower price. Fast-growing companies often have stratospheric P/Es, which is not a negative factor if that growth will continue. Earnings per share in most companies should be growing at the same rate as sales.

Dividends. Established companies pay dividends, which are calculated on a per-share basis. If a company pays a $1.00 per-share dividend, if you have 100 shares, you'll receive $100. In the annual report, scout *dividend growth.* Increasing dividends—issued every quarter by healthy companies—mean the company is able to share progressively more of its profits with investors. Companies without dividends aren't necessarily anathema to investors, but a steady record of dividend increases is desirable for long-term investors. Dividends mean stability and consistent profits. It's unusual for most growth companies to pay out more than half of their profits in dividends. In fact, most high-growth companies have paltry dividends. Nevertheless, for companies with a solid record of earnings and sales, dividends are an important component to watch.

Management Statements

The front section of every annual report contains the management's view of the past year and where the company is going. Managers comment on sales and earnings and how they came up with their numbers. They should also explain any negative factors such as loss of business, one-time earnings declines or write-offs, lawsuits (business sales, acquisitions, accounting problems), and other events that have an "adverse material impact" on the company's financial condition.

The second half of the report gives you "consolidated" financial statements and a shorter set of notes on certain accounting items. This is where you can get segment sales information, operating costs, tax information, and a whole host of detailed accounting numbers. I suggest you read the second half first; it contains much more detailed information and your mind won't be clouded by the glib "everything's coming up roses" commentary by managers in the first half of the report.

Generally, managers—particularly the CEO/chairman and division executives—put their numbers in the best possible light, but you want to know: 1) Will sales, earnings, or dividends continue to increase; 2) If not, why not, and for how long?

Back Matter

I often start at the back of a 10-K or annual report to dig for the bad news, because that's where it's often buried. A company must state if it's a defendant in a class-action suit and what their "exposure to liability" is in dollar terms, if that's available. Nearly every industrial company, for example, has some liability under the Superfund law (CERCLA) because they dumped some toxic waste on their facilities across the globe. Normally, this is not a devastating event (unless you're a concerned environmentalist or community where they dumped their waste). The nasty information you need to eye is anything to do with major consumer-driven class-action settlements. Several companies have filed for bankruptcy after these cases, especially if they made asbestos products, breast implants, or any products that harmed a lot of people (watch out for tobacco/food products companies).

Other gremlins to watch for involve "accounting irregularities," "one-time events," and other little items that pop up toward the end of an annual report or 10-K. You want the company to come clean on these little bugaboos. If their accounting problems are understated and have been going on for a while, that could lead to lowered earnings down the road, which depresses the stock price.

What You Need to Know: Basic Stock Analysis

Having read the annual report, the 10-K, and, I hope, *Value Line,* you're ready to crunch some numbers. So let's do some.

Sales (last five years including most recent year)	5-year Average Growth Rate	___
Net Income (same as above)	5-yr. Avg.	___
Earnings Per Share (same)	5-yr. Avg.	___
P/E Ratio	5-yr. Avg.	___

QUESTIONS ON WHETHER TO BUY

1. Are sales increasing at least 12%–15%/year?
2. Are profits increasing at least 12%–15%/year?
3. Do earnings per share follow the sales growth rate?
4. Is the current P/E at or near its 5-year average?

5. What are the negative factors in the management reports?
6. Based on the above, would you recommend this stock for long-term purchase?

Within your club (or by yourself), your answers above are the most boiled-down analysis a member should perform. There are literally hundreds of other calculations you can do to predict where a stock price might go, but for the purposes of just getting your feet wet, this is a good base. Naturally, this is not something you want to do during your first or second meeting. Even if you are on your own, you will need to familiarize yourself with annual reports, 10-Ks, and *Value Line*. Another essential resource is the nonprofit National Association of Investors Corporation's (NAIC) *Stock Selection Guide* and its *Starting and Running a Profitable Investment Club* (Times Books, 1998). I can't even attempt to duplicate the thoroughness of these two products. If you are serious about investment clubs or picking stocks, these publications are to beginning stock investors what hammers, nails, tape measures, and saws are to carpenters.

Where I part with the NAIC philosophy is on the complexity of their analysis and the alternative to doing it, that is, purchasing mutual funds. The NAIC only recently began covering and analyzing mutual funds, since its focus is on club stock investing. I believe that mutual funds can be the core of your portfolio and you only need a handful of funds (see chapter 8). Although nearly anybody can do a basic stock analysis, if you are not so inclined, you can build a well-diversified portfolio with mutual funds. Keep in mind that how you invest is a matter of your own personality, the amount of free time you have, and your willingness to do the work. If you can't spare the time to join a club and do stock research, then mutual funds might be a better vehicle for you. If you are interested in taking control of your finances, however, you'll clearly learn much more by picking your own stocks.

Stocks to Consider:
NAIC's Most Popular Stocks

Every year, the NAIC polls its membership, and participating clubs tell their mother organization about their favorite stocks. While not a scientific sampling, the NAIC Top 100 is a fairly good snapshot of the most popular stocks among investment clubs in North America. Most of the stocks on the list are familiar names: Wal-Mart, Coca-Cola, McDonald's. And some are lesser-known companies. Companies are on the list for one big reason: Their managements produce consistent earnings over time. The list is a great place to start when looking for companies to buy. Here are the top 50 stocks from the 1999 list to give you an idea of the kind of companies represented:

TOP 50 STOCKS HELD BY NAIC INVESTMENT CLUBS

1. Intel
2. Lucent
3. Home Depot
4. Cisco Systems
5. Merck
6. Pepsico
7. Microsoft
8. AFLAC
9. Pfizer
10. McDonald's
11. Diebold
12. Clayton Homes
13. Wal-Mart
14. Motorola
15. GE
16. Coca-Cola
17. AT&T
18. Oracle
19. Walt Disney
20. MCI Worldcom
21. Johnson & Johnson
22. Tricon Global
23. RPM
24. Walgreen's
25. Abbott Labs
26. Wendy's International
27. ADC Telecom
28. America Online
29. Amgen
30. Hewlett-Packard
31. EMC
32. Compaq
33. American Power Conversion
34. Staples
35. Medtronic
36. Century Telephone
37. Dell Computer
38. Synovus Financial
39. Harley-Davidson
40. Starbucks
41. Newell Rubbermaid
42. Citigroup
43. Southwest Airlines
44. Schlumberger
45. Sun Microsystems
46. Procter & Gamble
47. Exxon Mobil
48. Invacare
49. Boeing
50. Dollar General

Which Stocks We Picked and Why

In recent years, Wall Street has had a lovefest with technology stocks. So much so that companies with no earnings, little product, and very little chance of succeeding have enormous market capitalizations. Within our club—The Wall Street Prowlers—we recognize that technology will be a dominant force in the market for the next several decades, but we will only buy established companies with five-year records, at least 15% earnings growth, and dividend reinvestment plans. What we do is fairly typical for investment clubs, so I thought some of our stock-picking guidelines would be useful for you.

We stay away from start-ups because the truth about most of these companies is that they will fail—80% to 90% will go out of business. Although you can be optimistic about the Internet and the current technology boom, be realistic. That's why we focus on companies with at least five years' worth of earnings.

What will prosper in the next twenty years or so—when most traders are oriented toward the next twenty *seconds?* Before I give my opinion on that subject, let's do a history quiz. How many railroads that were exploding on the scene in the 1840s are still here? Remember the Pennsylvania Railroad? The New York Central? Most of them went bust and the others were absorbed into Conrail or bought out by the four goliath rail systems spanning the continent. Who made money investing in rails long term? Outside of the Wall Street "plungers" who ran up prices and dumped the stocks in panics they created, few investors can say rails made them rich. Like any great investing story, though, the silver lining of this cloud is usually right at your feet. Which companies really prospered during and *after* the rail boom? U.S. and Bethlehem Steel. Or any steel company that made the rails, the spikes, the ties, the switches, the boxcars, or the locomotives. I've personally witnessed mills and companies die as a business and labor reporter. It's degrading to communities and the families who depended on these lifeline industries. When investors lose interest, whole areas wither. It's like not watering or fertilizing a garden. But the rewards of cultivating down-to-earth investing are many splendored.

THE WALL STREET PROWLERS' PORTFOLIO

Stock	Industry
ADC Telecom	Telecom equipment
GE	Financial services, industrial products
Merck	Drugs, pharmacy benefit plans
Motorola	Cell phones, chips, electronics
Oracle	Database software
RPM	Coatings, paints
Sysco	Food service
Walgreen's	Drugstores

The upside of capitalism is that it rewards concerned and active investors—and investors who reinvest—with long-term returns, dividends, and continued growth. Most of those rewards come over time and are deeply rooted in often unglamorous basic products and services. One case in point is the General Electric Company. Formed by Thomas Edison originally to sell electricity, lightbulbs, and power-generation equipment, GE is a leading manufacturer of locomotives. Most of its customers may be long gone, but GE is still there, providing everything from financial services to washing machines (which is one reason the Prowlers picked GE).

Let's return to the current info-technology boom. This whole sea change in global business has a long way to go before it peaks. It's fueled by dramatic new ways of increasing productivity and reducing costs. Most of those technologies that deal with storing and exchanging information will fuel this explosion for decades. As a result, everything from shopping to cell phones will become faster, cheaper, and better. Our favorite candidate for the U.S. Steel of the information age is Oracle. Founded by Chicagoan Larry Ellison, this unglamorous company provides the rails, ties, and sidings for information. Their main business is database management systems and they are extremely good at it. Although they have lots of competition, their database management systems are the industry standard and continue to evolve. Long before the Internet was a twinkle in any computer user's eye, Oracle was showing the world how to efficiently store, retrieve, and manage huge amounts of information. For some reason, the stock was repositioned as a dot.com stock in 1999 and the price took off. Our club bought Oracle below $40 a share. One of our club members bought several hundred shares even cheaper and has been bragging ever since. Oracle will be laying a lot of track for the information age and its ride should be long and profitable.

Another stock that we don't see as a dot.com stock but is now being seen in a new light is Motorola. Kathleen and I have owned Motorola until we had to sell it from our personal portfolio to raise a down payment for a house. We had been accumulating Motorola in our DRIP (dividend reinvestment plan) for mostly under $60 a share. When it hit $170 after we sold it, my wife was not pleased, but fortunately she likes her new home.

Motorola is a scrappy company that keeps bouncing back from various mistakes and shifts in technology. A few years back, they nearly bet the farm on a cell phone standard that went nowhere while their Finnish and Japanese rivals were going digital. Now that they've figured that one out, Motorola is a leader again and will link its cell phones with Internet services. Not only that, Motorola makes set-top boxes for cable-TV Internet services, computer chips, radios, and lots of electronic components needed to run everything from dishwashers to microwaves. It's really a diversified electronics company that's an excellent innovator. Once CEO Christopher Galvin took over from his father, things started to roll. He's got an excellent business plan, reorganized the company, boosted marketing, and has Motorola going in the right direction. Of course, Motorola really goofed on Iridium and had a rough patch with Apple computers, but their exposures to those businesses was relatively small and it's forging ahead.

Motorola is a durable switch engine that's always waiting in the yard. Sometimes it pulls a big train and sometimes it's sitting on the siding waiting for another line of cars to pull. But it never sits around for long. Keep Motorola for a long time and you'll go places, too. For example, it split three-for-one on June 1, 2000.

Want another railroad-kind of stock for the information age? Here's another no-glamour company, which hardly makes headlines.

ADC Telecom, based in Minneapolis, makes digital switching systems. If you want to send information to and from a computer or telecom network, you need to switch it in and out. That's what ADC Telecom does, only they're involved with phone companies, cable companies, wireless providers, and just about anybody who has a signal to send. Like railroads, modern communication and the Internet simply won't run without switches and that's why ADC Telecom is a long-term buy.

Okay, so technology is wonderful and does great things to make our lives a little better. But it only represents 27% of the large companies (in the S&P 500 index) in the stock market. How about companies that actually save our lives? At the top of my list of lifesavers is Merck. Like Motorola, Merck has an excellent culture of innovation and research. It makes things that people need and want and is well managed. As one of the world's largest drug makers, Merck is up to the challenge of global drug research. They have a number of products in development based on genome research and they are going to do well with Vioxx, Singuliar, and Fosomax. Don't be scared about the government offering drugs as part of Medicare. That means more business for the drug makers, not less. Medicare will eventually be restructured to be more cost-effective, and drug therapies are the best way to go.

A Stock-Picking Philosophy: The HAT

Merck is a key player in what I call a HAT strategy that's good for any portfolio for the next twenty years. HAT is an acronym for Health, Aging, and Technology. All three will be impacting our economy as we age and become more productive over the next century. If you orient your portfolio toward these three trends, you will probably realize profitable results.

Speaking of getting old, a big play on aging is sitting right on the corner somewhere. Walgreen's is another stock that my wife and I sold to finance our new home, but it has a permanent place in our club portfolio. The reason why Walgreen's is a forever stock—or at least until people stop aging or getting sick—is because it's there. In some places, you can't drive more than three miles without seeing a bright Walgreen's on the corner. They switched from shopping center siting to stand-alones and are tremendously profitable. Although they were slow to capitalize on Internet sales, as usual Walgreen's waited and did it right. I think they'll outlast Amazon.com in this business. They finance internally, are building lots of stores, are in most states, and can give you a prescription no matter where you go. They are facing some good competition from CVS and Rite-Aid, but that will only make them better. You can buy anything from aspirin to radios in their stores. You walk in for drugs and walk out with milk, magazines, toys, and even radios. Walgreen's has the prescription for future growth.

A few other industry leaders I like include Sysco—the food service company, not the computer network firm—and RPM, the coatings manufacturer. I figure we'll all be eating and rusting in the future, so these well-managed companies are great long-term buys.

That's our club's portfolio for better or worse. We picked our stocks because they were leaders in their respective businesses, have resilient managements, and represent excellent long-term potential. Although I'm not recommending you buy these stocks, think ten or twenty years from now when you are eyeing a company. As with any stock you buy, the best perspective looks backward, forward, and sideways. See how your companies have done during slack periods for their industry. Have they bounced back? Were they worth holding over ten- or twenty-year periods (if they have been in business that long)? A durable portfolio will always have some down-on-their-luck companies, but if you've done your homework, they will rebound and reward you for your research and patience.

Now it's time to do your own research and add to your "common wealth." If you try stock-picking and decide it's not for you, read the next chapter to make your life simpler.

SUMMARY

1. Get some ideas on where to find good companies to buy.
2. Research the stocks for your club's consideration in your library.
3. Obtain essential information on stocks through *Value Line* and other sources.
4. Go through the annual reports and 10-Ks for more information.
5. Evaluate earnings, sales, and share price growth. Is it doubling in five years?
6. Make a decision for yourself or your club based on all of your information.

CHAPTER 7

A Regular Reward:
Reinvesting Dividends
and Buying More Shares

The Economics of Abundance means that there is an abundance of economists. In other words, the harder the times get, the harder the reading gets. It's a vicious circle. People who should be out purchasing something are sitting indoors reading an interpretive article in a magazine. (That goes for you, reader!) The more they read, the less they buy, and the less they buy, the sooner it's next month. Each month brings a new issue of the magazine, so where's the thing going to end? Or don't you care anymore?
—E. B. White, "Swing Low, Sweet Upswing,"
Quo Vadimus? (1939)

Morgantown, West Virginia, is as far as you can get from Wall Street, even though it's less than a day's drive away. Unlike many West Virginia towns, where King Coal once ruled, Morgantown had a diverse economy, with manufacturing and West Virginia University.

The Ten Buck Club was one investment club where anyone could do more than dream about a secure retirement. For ten to twenty dollars a month, you could buy stocks and one day have enough money to retire comfortably. Started at the University of West Virginia in Morgantown, the Ten Buck Club lived up to its name, getting several West Virginia U. faculty members started in stock-picking in 1956.

Gerald Eagan, an experienced member of the club, got involved in the 1980s, some thirty years after the club was founded. Eagan found that the club gave him more than ideas on which stocks to buy and allowed him to experiment on his own and move at his own pace.

"Members invested in multiples of $10 appropriate to their comfort level," Eagan recalls. "Most members felt it was a learning tool."

As a result of his club experience, Gerald set up his own IRAs, which included emerging growth stock funds and individual stocks. Through the club, he learned that the best long-term investment was held until the stock split, producing more shares, which were also held. The dividends were also reinvested in new shares. That way growth compounds over time, which builds additional wealth far into retirement.

Half of the twenty-seven current members of Ten Buck are retired, notes Steve Sanetrik, Ten Buck's current treasurer-agent (another term for treasurer). They range in age from thirty-five to ninety and all live in or near Morgantown. The club doesn't sell stocks very often, but each member is assigned a task, usually reviewing or suggesting stocks for sale or purchase.

The club is so old that none of the original members is left (it's one of the oldest in the United States), but the members easily reach quick consensus on most of their decisions. If stocks fail to perform—as Coca-Cola and Abbott Labs did recently—holdings are sold or reduced. It doesn't matter if a stock is volatile. They also monitor earnings per share, sales per share, share price, and debt, and check *Value Line* reports.

MONEY GROWS

Years	4%	6%	8%	10%
10	$1,481	$1,791	$2,159	$2,594
20	$2,191	$3,207	$4,661	$6,728
30	$3,243	$5,743	$10,063	$17,449

This chart shows the value of $1,000 compounded at various rates of return over time.

The Ten Buck portfolio speaks for itself as an example of how to diversify, reinvest, and build wealth over time. It embraces a number of industries. Of the eighteen stocks owned, there are only six losers (Allied Waste, Carlise, Diebold, Honeywell, Leggett & Platt, and Ross Stores), which may have turned around as this book goes to press. Use the Ten Buck portfolio to glean some ideas. I've included the average costs per share to give you some ideas of how these stocks were purchased. Look up the current prices as you read this and see how they've done. Members pooled cash dividends with continuous monthly investments to buy 100-share round lots. The best stock purchases have increased through splits. This is a surprisingly neglected model for buying stocks: to find growing companies at great prices, *hold* them, and reinvest new shares and dividends in additional shares or new stocks.

TEN BUCK CLUB PORTFOLIO

Stock	Cost per Share
Abbott Labs	14.47
Allied Waste	10.40
Applied Material	12.84
Becton Dickenson	6.31
Carlise	43.18
Cisco Systems	13.06
Citigroup	29.85
Coca-Cola	4.87
Diebold	25.90
General Electric	39.90
Home Depot	5.77
Honeywell	51.47
Leggett & Platt	26.19
Merck	21.97
Ross Stores	19.68
Transocean Offshore	21.84
Xilinx	43.93
Y-Alliance	1.00

The Importance of Dividend-Reinvestment Plans

I'm assuming by now you've garnered some ideas on a savings plan and have your money market fund parking your money better than a valet at a high-priced restaurant. You've sampled the potatoes or pasta. How about some meat? This section will tell you some easy entrees for your first investment meals.

In this age of the Internet and hyper-growth companies, why bother with the concept of a dividend? After all, the lion's share of high-flying companies in high technology don't bother with them. Aren't dividends a vestige of the smokestack era of investing? What role do dividends play in a time when capital appreciation (growth in the market value of a stock) is propelling the market to even greater heights? These are all valid questions any serious investor must face, no matter what time they are investing.

Back in the days before capital appreciation was the order of the day, there was the dividend. A dividend is simply a cash payment that represents a portion of profits. Companies wanted to keep shareholders interested over long periods of time, so every quarter they cut checks to their investors. A dividend is like sugar on top, a little reward for sticking with a company. Dividends also lend some stability to a stock. Stock prices go up and down every second of the trading day, but dividends are meant to be on a constant and an ever-upward path. The market may punish a stock's price in a number of ways, but most companies don't slash their dividends unless they are in deep trouble.

Dividends are an important component of the *total return* of a stock. The main component for stocks is capital appreciation, or the amount a stock's price goes up. Combine the dividend with capital appreciation—how much the stock price increases—and you have *total return.* Unlike a stock price, a dividend is found money, even if the stock price goes down. Of course, companies may cut dividends, but only at their own peril. When a stock is depressed, dividends often provide the only return. You'll get a check even though a stock is in the dump.

A dividend is generally expressed as so many dollars or cents a share. To find out how much you'll receive, simply multiply the dividend times the number of shares you own. If you have 100 shares of a stock and it pays a $1 a share, then you'll have $100 coming. You can figure out a stock's dividend *yield* by taking the dividend and dividing by the current share price. Generally, if dividends stay the same and the stock price rises, the yield will fall and vice versa. It's a simple percentage that shows you what proportion of the stock price is being paid as the dividend.

As a rule, the more established companies pay a dividend. Young companies usually are pouring every dollar into growing their business—building plants, marketing, etc.—and don't have the spare cash to pay dividends. Older, more mature companies that pay dividends may not have as much upside as younger companies do in their stock price, but they can make up for it by paying a hefty dividend.

Some of the oldest companies pay the healthiest dividends. Most utilities, which were established in the late nineteenth and early twentieth centuries, pay dividends. General Electric, which began as a producer and distributor of electricity, for example, has paid a dividend every year since 1899. Pharmaceutical companies are also known for their generous dividends. Recently Real Estate Investment Trusts, which are stock corporations that buy commercial property and mortgages, also had high dividends. Of course, how high a dividend is depends on what industry a company is in. A 3% dividend yield for a utility would be embarrassing, but extremely generous for a bank (see box below for an example of dividend ranges). You can find any company's dividend by looking in the stock listings of any newspaper: They're under the column headed "DIV."

Dividends as Insurance

Dividends should not be confused with a company's growth potential, nor should they be the only reason you buy a stock. A company can have a great dividend, but questionable upside potential in its price. Philip Morris and several utilities are good cases in point. They may pay generous dividends, but may not offer you

STOCKS WITH HIGH DIVIDENDS

Company	Industry	Dividend Yield*
Bob Evans Farms	Food	2.3%
Central Southwest	Utility	8.7%
Dillard's	Retail	0.8%
First Midwest Banc	Banking	4.5%
Hasbro	Toys	1.4%
Mercury General	Insurance	3.8%
Pep Boys	Auto parts, repair	3.0%
Philip Morris	Food, tobacco	8.0%
Wallace Computer	Tech services	4.1%
Wausau-Mosinee	Paper	2.9%

Source: Investment Quality Trends newsletter, 7440 Girard Ave., Suite 4, La Jolla, CA 92037.

*Dividend yields at time of publication. Although these examples are not necessarily recommended, they show the wide range of yields from industry to industry.

much capital appreciation; in fact, the opposite may be true. As an investor, your primary objective is still growth. Dividends are the little bonuses that are worth having, but not the sole objective in buying a stock, unless, of course, you need a portfolio that is designed to produce mostly income.

Most savvy investors know that dividends provide a bit of an insurance policy for stocks in bear markets. During large sell-offs, stocks with dividends generally hold up better (price-wise) than those without. That's because investors know, at the very least, that they have that dividend paying cash no matter what the stock price does. Capital gains come and go, but a consistent dividend is a buoy, not an anchor, in a stormy market.

A famous study by Cornell University found that in the crash of October 1987, stocks *without* dividends plunged 36%, while stocks *with* dividends dipped only 32%. That reduced loss may not sound like much, but if you compared two $10,000 portfolios (one with

KITCHEN-TABLE TIP

DIVIDENDS BOOST RETURNS OVER TIME

You're naturally leery about those gasps in the market when there seems to be no bottom. What's going to make your money grow over time when there's such volatility? Consider that over fifteen-year periods measured over the last 60 years by Ibbotson Associates, a portfolio of stocks made money every time. But you would not have made money if you did not invest all your dividends. Overall, you lost money only 11% of the time. The moral: The longer you invest, the lower the risk, especially when all dividends are reinvested.

dividend-paying stocks and one without), the dividend-rich portfolio would have been worth $1,080 more than the non-dividend mix. So you're better off, in a safety sense, with at least some dividend-producing stocks in your portfolio to provide some security during downturns.

Reinvesting Dividends: Just Do It

Unless you need the income, the best use of a dividend is reinvesting it. Enter the dividend-reinvestment plan (DRIP), one of the best inventions since the advent of compound interest. The modern DRIP is the modern equivalent of the nuclear breeder reactor. Companies paying dividends pay them in new shares, which are automatically bought and invested in a DRIP.

The best DRIPs not only reinvest dividends in new shares but provide for "optional cash payments," which is a way of buying even more stock directly through the company—without using a broker or paying a commission.

As an investing tool, the DRIP is to long-term investors what a power saw is to a carpenter. It does the hard work for you. You don't have to make a phone call, write a check (unless you are buying new shares), or even transfer money. Companies with DRIPs use "transfer agents," which are generally banks, to process all of their transactions.

If you want to buy new shares, you send a check to the transfer agent and they will buy the shares and place them in your account. You can even set up automatic debits from checking, savings, and money market accounts to buy new shares. No sweat. No hassle.

If you get 5% yield (that's halfway between zero and 10% on the highest-yielding stocks), that's nearly half of the 11% historical return of the S&P 500 over the last sixty-six years or so. That means even mediocre capital gains of 6% get you half of what a S&P 500 stock index fund would do—and you didn't really have to do much to achieve this.

Reinvesting Mutual Funds Dividends

Even if you have a portfolio consisting only of mutual funds (see chapter 8), you can still reinvest dividends. With funds, you have an option to receive "distributions"—mutual fund parlance for dividends and capital gains—in direct payment at the end of the year or have them reinvested. Check the box on the fund application to "reinvest dividends." That way, your gains and dividends will be buying more shares at a lower price. The fund goes "ex-dividend" in December to pay out distributions. Gains will be paid out, if there are any—the share price drops by the per share amount of the distribution. Thus you can buy more shares of the fund *automatically* at a lower price. Outside of a tax-deferred vehicle like an IRA, you'll pay taxes on your distribution, so make sure you have your IRAs and similar plans fully funded.

How to Get Started with DRIPs

To get started, first you'll need to pick a stock to buy. You can move on from there, but it will be rewarding if this first stock pays a regular dividend. One share will get you started. You can buy it any of three ways:

▪ **Through Direct-Investment Plans (DIPs).** Companies sell stock directly, so you can get the first and subsequent shares directly through them without going through a broker. Not only do you bypass the broker's commission, you're immediately enrolled in the company's DRIP. So your first dividend payment—and all others from then on—are reinvested in new shares, even if they are fractional shares. Although there are less than 1,000 companies with DRIPs, the list is growing every day. Some are big names like McDonald's and Texaco.

• **Buy one share through a discount broker in your name (or your club's), then transfer that share into the company's DRIP.** First, you have to determine if the company has a DRIP. If they don't, that's not always a problem (move on to the next option). Find the lowest-commission broker available, open a brokerage account, buy one share, then instruct the broker to transfer the share into the company's DRIP.

• **Buy shares through special services.** These services exist to serve investors like you and are generally low cost and handle the initial paperwork. All you need is the money for one share and pay a small service fee or modest commission (under $10). The services are listed at the end of this chapter.

Consistent Reinvestment Is the Game Plan

Once you have bought your shares, you can add to them every month—either by writing a check or through automatic debits. This puts your stock purchase plan on "autopilot." You also avoid price extremes by dollar-cost averaging. This is how it works: Say you consistently invest $10 in new shares through a DRIP in stock X. Here's your average cost through a year:

DOLLAR-COST AVERAGING

Month	Cost Per Share
January	$40
February	$42
March	$38
April	$36
May	$30
June	$35

DOLLAR-COST AVERAGING *(continued)*

Month	Cost Per Share
July	$40
August	$43
September	$48
October	$52
November	$49
December	$41

Average Cost Per Share = $41.16

As you can see, by employing dollar-cost averaging you are neither buying at the highest price nor the lowest price. To make this strategy work, you need to have picked a stock that has consistent earnings and solid management. When a stock splits, you get more shares and you can buy at a lower price, thus lowering your overall cost.

A Drawback to DRIPs and DIPs

The one drawback about DRIPs and DIPs is that they produce a tremendous amount of paperwork and you rarely have a choice as to when the purchase is made. With some plans, such as those operated through the National Association of Investors Corp. (NAIC), your purchase may be made a month or more after you send in the paperwork. So if you had your eye on an especially low price, you may not get it right on the mark. You can also get derailed at tax time if you have sold a stock (as my wife and I did with Motorola) and are missing some paperwork that helps you calculate your "basis" for owning the stock—and figuring capital gains taxes.

The clear alternative to DRIPs and DIPs offered by companies is going through brokers who offer DRIPs (see next page). They can consolidate your paperwork and buy the day you send in a buy order. They are slightly more expensive in terms of nominal fees, but they may be worth it for the convenience and getting the price you want.

Dividend Reinvestment Resources

As I mentioned, there are several ways of investing in DRIPs and DIPs. Nearly 100 plans offer discounts on reinvested dividends. Not only do you automatically buy new shares with your "optional" cash payments, you get a break on the new shares. Nearly two-thirds of the plans have a "no cost" feature to buy new shares. That means $100 buys $100 of new shares without deductions for commissions or administrative fees. Some plans offer perks to shareholders. For example, Anheuser-Busch, the brewery company, offers DRIPs and DIPs. You can also buy American Depository Receipts, which are foreign stocks listed on American exchanges. The following services will get you started:

American Association of Individual Investors, www.aaii. com, 800-428-2244. This membership organization publishes *Individual Investors Guide to Dividend Reinvestment Plans* and provides low-cost entry into direct-investment plans.

BuyandHold.com, www.buyandhold.com. A service that provides online access to hundreds of plans.

Direct Investing, www.directinvesting.com. A large group of direct-investment and dividend-reinvestment plans.

The DRIP Investor, www.dripinvestor.com, 219-852-3200. The online newsletter suggests stocks and portfolios for long-term investors and is a good place to start before you sign up with one of the other services.

Moneypaper/Temper of the Times, www.drp.com, 800-388-9993. A service that provides access to more than 200 plans. Also see www.moneypaper.com.

National Association of Investors Corporation, www. better-investing.org. The NAIC, the nonprofit group behind more than 250,000 investment clubs, provides two plans that allow you to invest in companies directly. Their Low-Cost investment plan is popular among investment clubs and is available to members. They also have another plan that invests in stocks that typically don't offer DRIPs on their own.

Netstock Direct, www.netstock.com. Offers a "ShareBuilder" program that allows you to invest in company DRIPs online. There are no minimum investments and you can store your records and portfolio online. Also see www.sharebuilder.com.

Universal Stock Access Account, www.u-s-a-account.com, 800-295-2550. Provides low-cost access to more than 250 stocks. The USA account also features companies that normally don't offer DRIPs.

The Directory of Companies Offering Dividend Reinvestment Plans (16th Edition) is published annually by Evergreen Enterprises. It's a fairly comprehensive list of dividend-reinvestment plans and what they offer.

SUMMARY

1. Know the importance of dividends as wealth builders and safeguards.
2. Buy shares through specialized DRIPs or DIPs.
3. Take advantage of services that offer DRIPs and DIPs. Buy one share to begin.
4. Reinvest your dividends in new shares.
5. Dollar-cost average to buy new shares.

CHAPTER 8

The Million-Dollar Portfolio: Supplementing Your Nest Egg with Mutual Funds

Each small task of everyday life is part of the total harmony of the universe.

—St. Thérèse of Lisieux

Quentin Sampson jokes that his wife said she was going to leave him when he decided to take his retirement funds in one lump sum in 1992. After thirty-five years of working with People's Gas in Chicago as a computer technician, he easily could have taken the safe route and left his money in the company plan. What could be safer than a gas company pension plan for a man of sixty-two?

Having had a taste of investment clubbing through a group he joined through work, he was eager to invest on his own, buying shares through DRIPs and reinvesting the dividends and buying new shares. Like the legion of investment clubbers funding their nest eggs through DRIPs, he followed the rules: He only bought companies with five years of earnings history that were growing around 15% a year.

A few years before he retired, however, he decided to share the wealth of his knowledge. He started a family investment club, proposing no minimum investment, but suggesting $10 a month as a contribution. Family members from three months to seventy years were enrolled, from grandparents to great-grandchildren, from Denver to Atlanta.

He also shared his wealth with clubs he helped form in the south suburbs of Chicago, eventually mentoring a "model club" in Harvey, Illinois, which is an open club for novices. The twenty-five-member club meets in the Harvey library and covers basic stock investing skills for a predominantly African-American membership. The rules are clear: Attend at least four meetings or you're asked to leave, and no one person can own more than 15% of club holdings. There are many dropouts, but those who stay learn how to invest on their own. All stocks are bought for reinvestment in DRIPs.

"The [model] club is open to the public, anyone who wants to learn what it's all about is welcome," Quentin says. "This club is sort of the mother lode. If people do their research, they go off and form their own clubs."

U.S. HOUSEHOLDS THAT OWN MUTUAL FUNDS, 1980–1999*

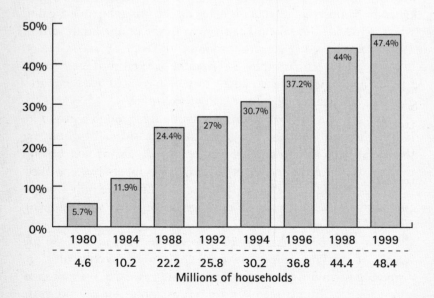

Source: ICI.

It's not unusual for clubs to compound their knowledge for their members, then spawn new clubs. It's the nature of investment knowledge to replicate itself like DNA. Quentin even keeps an inventory of shares of stock that he sells to clubs so that they can get started without having to go through a broker. His wealth helps others build theirs.

Quentin is diligent about keeping his stocks. He'll only sell shares if he needs the money and he's only sold five companies since he started investing. "The most difficult part is selling, but we eliminate that by *not* selling."

For Quentin, investing is not only a family affair, it's something that bonds him to other people as they learn how to generate their New Prosperity. One of his yearly family events is attending the Berkshire-Hathaway annual meeting in Omaha with his son, David, where he gets to meet with investment sage Warren Buffett.

"Warren Buffett shook David's hand and after that he decided to go back to college," Quentin recalls. "African-Americans and most minorities are not investing in the stock market at the same rates as whites. I've catered strongly to young people because their parents know nothing about investing."

TECHNOLOGY STOCKS GOOD FOR "WILD CARDS"

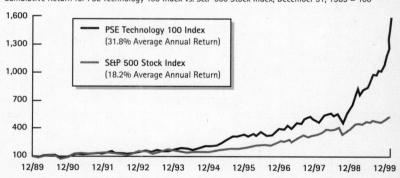

Technology Strong over Last Decade

Cumulative Return for PSE Technology 100 Index vs. S&P 500 Stock Index, December 31, 1989 = 100

- PSE Technology 100 Index (31.8% Average Annual Return)
- S&P 500 Stock Index (18.2% Average Annual Return)

Source: S&P 500 Stock Index, Pacific Stock Exchange Technology Index.

As an NAIC director and inspirational leader for many clubs, Quentin is a believer in the dogma of the investment club movement. He will analyze stocks using *Value Line* and *Standard & Poor's* and look for quality management that delivers earnings growth, sales, and relatively low price-to-earnings ratios. All told, he needs ten to fifteen reasons to buy a stock before he signs up with the DRIP.

Although his personal portfolio consists of up to eighty companies, Quentin supplements his stock holdings by owning mutual funds. He owns an international stock and an index fund, which consist of half of his retirement holdings (the other half is in individual stocks). His largest holdings include:

QUENTIN SAMPSON'S PORTFOLIOS (A PARTIAL LISTING)

Stock	**Industry**
Berkshire Hathaway	Insurance, diversified
People's Energy	Gas utility
McDonald's	Restaurants
Motorola	Cell phones, electronics
IBM	Computers, software

HARVEY MODEL CLUB

Walgreen's	Drugstores
Intel	Chips
Motorola	Cell phones
AT&T	Long-distance phones
Paycheck	Payroll processors

FAMILY CLUB

Wal-Mart	Retail
AFLAC	Insurance
McDonald's	Food
Disney	Entertainment
GTE	Telephone service

Quentin Sampson's portfolios are only part of his investment picture. His holdings in mutual funds round out his stock investments. For example, he invested in an international mutual fund to give him overseas exposure and lower his overall risk in the U.S. stock market. In case there are any high-growth companies he missed on his own, he's holding the Vanguard 500 Stock Index mutual fund.

What if you have neither the time nor the inclination to do what Quentin has done with his portfolio and clubs? Mutual funds are the simple answer.

What If You Don't Want to Pick Stocks?

If you're pulling your hair out by now—and have said to yourself, "There's *no way* I'll have the time to pick individual stocks"—this is the chapter for you. How would you like to just stick your money in one place and leave it there for twenty or thirty years? Does such a vehicle exist? In mutual funds, not only do long-term growth vehicles thrive, they do almost all the work for you. There's little doubt that mutual funds are the best friends an investor could have. They pool money so that you don't have to go out and buy hundreds of stocks on your own. They offer professional management at a relatively low cost. And they offer you so many ways to invest, small wonder why they are so popular.

With more than 6,000 funds on the market, however, the process of selecting them can be daunting. After all, they are offered by everyone from American Airlines to Zurich-Kemper. And then there are the funds offered through pension programs like 401(k)s and 403(b)s. The sheer number of them is bewildering.

What the fund industry (except for a handful of companies) doesn't want you to know is that there is a blissfully simple way of choosing them. There are few secrets in mutual funds, since they are monitored by the U.S. Securities and Exchange Commission and you can find out about them on the Internet, in the public library, and in every newspaper. There are as ubiquitous as gas stations.

It always amazes me to what degree different financial publications will go to review the latest, newest, and hottest funds. Like

> ## KITCHEN-TABLE TIP
>
> ### WHY YOU SHOULDN'T INVEST IN LAST YEAR'S HOT FUND
>
> You just won't get last year's return. It's better to stick to a "total market" stock index fund that covers the Wilshire 5000 index. Over the past decade, this index beat 72% of all U.S. stock funds. So a stock index mutual fund is the first place you should start when you start any retirement plan.

most investors' approach to stocks, the conventional wisdom is generally wrong. This is what you need to know.

Portfolio Pillars: The Four Essential Funds

You can cover the best growth stocks in the world by owning just four mutual funds. This will drive most mutual fund marketing mavens crazy, but it's the truth. You'll not only get away with owning four mutual funds, you'll save thousands of dollars in management and sales fees and be diversified with companies across the world. Funds that invest in an "index" of stocks essentially hold the stocks and never sell them. They are also managed for up to one-tenth of what "managed" funds charge investors, so you boost your total return because you are paying reduced management expenses.

With index funds, you don't have to worry about whether they "beat the market" every year, because they represent entire markets. The popular Standard & Poor's 500 Index is the standard every growth stock fund manager tries to beat, although three quarters of them don't. So if you can't beat the index, why not *own* it?

Index funds representing the Wilshire 5000 index, which comprises nearly every listed stock on U.S.-based exchanges, are the best vehicles to "own" the majority of stocks in the NYSE, NASDAQ, AMEX, and regional exchanges. The principle behind the fund is simple: A manager buys all 5,000 stocks and doesn't sell. You get the return of all of those stocks plus whatever dividends they pay minus a paltry management fee.

With the Wilshire 5000, you get everything from Coca-Cola to the tiniest technology start-up that lists its stock on an exchange. What's remarkable about this index is that you don't need to worry if the manager owns the stocks that are going to be hot that year. Since they have most of the stocks that are listed, they have the highfliers already in the portfolio. Even if you are lucky enough to be in a sizzling fund—or pick the stocks yourself—once you subtract brokerage costs and taxes, there's almost no way you can beat an index.

The second fund in your stable is one that stakes you in the rest of the world. International index funds give you the top companies in Europe, Asia, and Latin America. These funds work on the same principle as the Wilshire 5000, only they buy stocks you may not have access to and offer worldwide diversification.

A third fund worth having involves a different style of stock-picking called *value investing*. Unlike growth-oriented investors who focus on earnings growth, value managers pick stocks based on their relative value to their "book" value—what a company is worth if it's liquidated. Though value investing has been out of favor for the last few years, it doesn't hurt to have bargain stocks in your portfolio when there's a prolonged downturn.

Rounding out your portfolio you'll buy what I call the "wild card" of the deck. This is an aggressive fund that may focus exclusively on one industry or sector of the economy, but produce above-average returns. These "sector" funds invest in anything from telecommunications to health care and are also good for the long term, only they will be more volatile from year to year. They will pump up returns considerably when they are in favor.

Each fund gives you a different part of the stock market and seeks to cover your bases by pooling the resources of the funds. All you have to do is fill out the applications and send in the checks (or wire the money). Every one of these funds can be part of IRAs or company plans, so you can set them up yourself in a few minutes. Although most investment clubs focus on individual stocks, there's no reason you can't invest in a mutual fund, too.

RECOMMENDED FUNDS

Fund	Type	5 yr. Tot. Return	(800) Number
Vanguard Total Market Index	Wilshire index	26.8%	662–7447
Vanguard Total International Index	International index	29.9%*	662–7447
Vanguard Small Cap Value Index	Value index	17.05%†	662–7447
T. Rowe Price Science & Tech	Wild card/tech	39.45%	541–8803

OTHER WILD CARD FUNDS TO CONSIDER

Fund	Type	5 yr. Tot. Return	(800) Number
Fidelity Select Electronic	Technology	54.55%	544–8888
Vanguard Health Care	Health care	29.37%	662–7447
Davis NY Venture	Value	25.10%	279–0279

* The Vanguard funds are chosen because they are typically the lowest-cost index funds in the business.

†Equals 1-year return; 5-year return not available since the fund is relatively new.

Neat Things You Can Do with Mutual Fund Families

Like most financial services providers, mutual fund companies or "families" are tripping over themselves to offer you extra services once you're in the door. They all have Web sites and offer some of their best services at little or no cost. Most of these services take the form of online software, or "calculators," which will permit you to make complex calculations without buying expensive software. Of course, every major mutual fund company offers brokerage, money management, annuities, and retirement planning services. Here's a sampling:

Fidelity, www.fidelity.com. Offers online retirement-planning software.

Strong, www.estrong.com. Online newsletter and calculator on investing lump sums.

T. Rowe Price, www.troweprice.com. Offers college and retirement-planning software.

Vanguard, www.vanguard.com. After-tax returns and fund-costs calculators.

What If You Can Only Invest Small Amounts?

This is not really a problem. Although most funds want you to pony up anywhere from $2,000 to $10,000 to open an account, the following fund families will let you invest with smaller sums of money.

MUTUAL FUNDS WITH LOW INITIAL INVESTMENTS

Fund Group = $500 or Less	(800) Number
Columbia	547–1707
Dreyfus	373–9387
Fidelity	544–8888
Gabelli	422–3554
Invesco	525–8085
Janus	525–8983
Jones & Babson	422–2766
Neuberger & Berman	877–9700
Nicholas	227–5987
T. Rowe Price	638–5660
Schwab	435–4000
Strong	368–1030
TIAA-CREF	223–1200
USAA	382–8722

SUMMARY

1. Pick stocks, but know what you are missing in terms of diversification.
2. Pick stock mutual funds to cover all of your bases.
3. Choose stock index funds to cover entire markets and regions.
4. Choose "wild cards" to enhance returns.

CHAPTER 9

Fine-Tuning Your Kitchen-Table Plan: How to Stay the Course and Know When to Sell

If money is flowing, then it's healthy money, a healthy system. The Chinese ideogram for money is a spring, the same as a water spring. Actually, currency comes from the word current, *which is a flow. Money is, in that sense, a little like blood.*

—Jacob Needleman

Ilene Matteson was a little jet-lagged when I asked her about her intergenerational Outlook Investment Club. She had just come back from a trip to China, where she "ate more rice than I care to eat for another year." She had always wanted to visit the country, as a reader of Marco Polo's adventures and collector of Chinese art and objects. A previously planned trip had been canceled due to the Tiananmen Square massacre, so this was a special trip, even though her husband, John, had passed away since they first scheduled it.

One of the last activities she undertook with her husband was starting a family investment club. They had seen the Beardstown Ladies on *60 Minutes* and they both thought it was a good idea to get the family together. Although they lost nine out of their sixteen original members, it was a going concern by late 1995.

The youngest members of the club were allowed to put in as little as $5 a month; the minimum for the adults was $25. The ages ranged from a six-year-old to Ilene's 83-year-old sister, Tillie. Ilene took kids to the library, taught them how to research stocks and use the computer.

As a retired human resources manager for Metropolitan Life, Ilene was well prepared for her retirement through 401(k) company plans, IRAs, and mutual funds. As a result of her preparation, she was able to retire at 56 and move to be closer to her family in the Denver area. At retirement, though, she had a feeling that she could manage her money better herself.

"We received a small inheritance when we retired," Ilene remembers. "So we contributed $4,000 to the family members in our club for investment. Why should we let others handle the money? Why can't we do it ourselves?"

The first investments were made into stock DRIP plans. The kids invested little amounts such as $1 they were given by their parents to buy ice cream or Christmas gift money. "Kids are like sponges; by the time they are teens, they will be investors."

THE OUTLOOK INVESTMENT CLUB

Stock	Industry
Amgen	Biotechnology
AT&T	Long-distance phones
Clayton Homes	Manufactured housing
Lucent	Telecom equipment
McDonald's	Food
Pepsico	Food, beverages
State Street	Mutual fund transfer agent
Wal-Mart	Retail

Now every holiday is an occasion for saving and investing. The kids get $25 for birthdays and they learn about investing and e-mail ideas to Ilene. "They're just so into this, you can't believe it."

Of course, the family club has hit roadblocks. Like most clubs, it loathes selling stocks. It's like an admission of failure when they have to unload a company after doing all of their research and hoping to

SHORT-TERM TRADERS LOSE BIG

The perils of day trading

A National American Securities Administrators Association (NASAA) study in August 1999 investigated day trading. Here's what they found:

70% of day traders will lose nearly all their money.

Fewer than **12%** of day traders made a profit on their short-term trades.

67 out of **68** accounts at a day trading branch lost money.

hold it forever. They had to sell Tricon Global—a food service concern spun off from Pepsico that owns franchises like Taco Bell—after sales disappointed the club. "Believe me, selling Tricon was almost a gut-wrenching experience because we had never sold a stock!" To date, that one sale has not hampered the club. On a total investment of some $22,000, the club's portfolio is worth more than $40,000.

As a club or individual you will reach that crossroads: Buy or *sell.* It's often the most difficult decision you make because you have committed to a buy-and-invest strategy. Fortunately, there are some solid guidelines to know when to pull the trigger on a wayward stock or fund.

Another Prowlers Saga

Like the Outlook Club, my own family club, the Wall Street Prowlers, presented a number of challenges in deciding when to buy a long-term stock. Although our decision to buy stocks is usually a smooth transaction, that's not always the case. That was the story with our discussion to buy General Electric. After all, this was the most "admired company" of 1998 and 1999, at least according to

Fortune magazine. It was also my idea; I was beaming with the promise of having found *El Dorado,* the one stock that could do it all and produce great returns over time. So I made my case to the club.

I presented GE to the club after Martin, my brother-in-law, presented Charles Schwab, a brokerage with a leading online operation, that just bought U.S. Trust to get into the trust account management business, and was good at everything it did. But Martin panned GE because of its lofty stock price and P/E at the time, even after a market dip. As he read his wrinkled *Value Line* sheets, Martin turned up his nose at the idea of buying Schwab at current prices, even though another sell-off the previous week had trimmed Schwab stock price some 43%. But at a P/E ratio of 64.6%, we were not getting any bargain, so we moved on. That opened the door for my presentation.

We had been struggling for nearly a year to find a stock in the financial services business and dispensed with a number of banks, finance companies, and conglomerates such as Citicorp. We had gone through at least a half-dozen companies, but each had a huge Achilles heel in being overpriced or having uneven earnings or poor management. We needed a breakthrough for our meager portfolio, which was becoming dominated by technology and health products and services (Motorola, Oracle, ADC Telecom, Walgreen's).

Enter GE, which, after the market collapse of mid-April 2000, overtook Microsoft as the mostly highly valued company in the world. At more than $330 billion (outstanding shares multiplied by its share price at the time), GE was a player in nearly everything, but to me its best segment was in financial services. Its Capital Services division was a business unto itself, generating $1 billion in profit alone. This division leases equipment, jet aircraft, provides credit cards, and even manages mutual funds and sells insurance. By itself, the division accounted for more than 40% of GE's profits and was the jewel in the crown.

I even loved the wonderful history of the company, which has been cutting dividend checks for 101 straight years. Thomas Edison bid his chief assistant Samuel Insull to create the company so that Edison could market his inventions, build power plants to power them, and be free to go back to his lab and invent more. I had even seen two of Sam Insull's houses and admired him, even though Insull died a disgraced tycoon alone on a Paris park bench after the market crash of 1929.

STOCK PROFILE: GE

Price Range (1999): $99.81–$164.88
P/E Ratio (avg. 5 yrs.): 50
Businesses: Aircraft engines, appliances, Capital Services, industrial systems, information services, lighting, medical systems, NBC/CNBC, plastics, power systems, transportation systems.

Aside from financial services, I pitched GE as a diversified industrial company. It is the world's leading manufacturer of jet engines, gas turbines, and power plant equipment—all growth industries. You already know about the lightbulbs, appliances, NBC network and CNBC cable stations. As if that weren't enough, the company also makes medical systems (CAT/MRI scanners), plastics, and supplies technical services. This was no Internet start-up, although GE was just getting into e-commerce to sell its thousands of products more efficiently. The company was even going to split three-for-one, making the shares even more affordable for our piquant stock-buying budget. So what's not to like? Then the lightning bolt struck.

Steve Beicos, a former engineer and our most analytical member, had to ask only one question: What's the upside potential—how much could we expect the stock to appreciate? This was a perfectly valid question, since clubs (and most sensible investors) should invest in companies to make money over time. By my calculations, the company would grow from 7% to 10%, including the 1.05% dividend yield. It was very close to its all-time high of $164.88, and had a lofty P/E of 50 over the last five years, making GE an expensive stock to buy. I could not deny the numbers, so I parried with the idea that GE was not fully realizing potential earnings from its gas turbine business—a growing, relatively clean and efficient way of producing electricity. Nor was this industrial colossus saying anything about selling NBC or partnering with some major Internet player, which it had yet to do. More profits not on the books now.

So Steve ran his numbers and came up with little possible appreciation for my beloved GE. "I can buy a long-term [Treasury] bond and get a better return," he said with alacrity. "Why would I want to buy this stock if it's not going up that much?"

I reinforced my best arguments for the company. Yes, Steve's numbers were correct, but there were many things not reflected in the numbers. These were *qualitative* issues, such as growth not reflected in anyone's current or future predictions. Their Internet presence would grow, their power business would grow, they would sell more aircraft engines and more consumer financial services.

After Kathleen and Martin supported me—and loved the idea of a three-for-one split and accumulating shares for years to come at lower prices—Steve was unconvinced and unmoved. The numbers were on his side. The investment club orthodoxy is that if you can't buy a company that grows at 15% a year, or doubles in five, don't buy it. There are other companies out there. We picked Oracle, ADC Telecom, and Motorola because they were growing at least that much. Oracle took a huge jump after we bought it, as did ADC Telecom. Both were long-term buys even though they became expensive after we bought them.

Our club tabled the idea of buying GE that month. Fortunately, we had another stock we all liked waiting in the wings. We bought twenty shares of Merck instead, which was trading at $66 a share, had an extremely reasonable P/E of 27, and was well off its high of $81. We unanimously agreed that Merck was a good buy, out of favor, and deserved our attention. Besides, as one of the largest drug companies in the world, it would eventually be recognized, develop new drugs, and help heal the ills of aging Americans. Which brings us to the idea of thinking long term.

The meeting following my GE presentation, Steve did his own analysis of GE and found that it *could* show up to 15% appreciation, if all the other factors we discussed continued on course. So we bought $250 worth through GE's direct-investment plan. Our argument had compelled us to do some more homework. There was nothing personal in our difference of opinion: Steve and I have been friends for twenty-five years. We just took another look at the numbers as *investors*. This process was a hallmark for us, however. We were looking at stocks not because we liked what the company did— but for what they could produce in terms of total return. If you accept no other challenge from investing on your own or with a club, if you shoot for total return, you'll be successful. Sometimes, though, you just need to take a critical second look before you invest.

When It's Time to Say No

Our little impasse over GE was typical in investment club settings. It happens frequently when investors love stocks but want to ignore the numbers. I suppose the dynamic would have been different if Steve were a family member, but I welcomed his rational approach, which tempers possible bad investment decisions. You need to see the other side of an argument. There are thousands of companies that are great ideas for businesses, but they may not be profitable enough or their stocks so overvalued you may need to wait until you buy them. In short, you need to know how to say no and take your time. Here are guidelines on how to evaluate a stock with that in mind:

SAYING NO AS A SMART INVESTOR: GUIDELINES

1. Look at the company's price range. Is it near the high end of its fifty-two-week range? If so, ask why its price is so high.
2. Although the P/E ratio is important, keep in mind that earnings always support growth in the stock price. The higher the P/E, the less likely earnings are there to prop up the price. That makes a stock more vulnerable to a decline if the market turns south. Of course there are plenty of Internet companies with no earnings and insane P/Es, but the "efficient market theory" holds that sooner or later investors will realize that if the earnings aren't there, the price can't be supported.

3. Where is the growth coming from? If the company—or its various businesses—aren't growing at around 15% or better in terms of revenues and profits, then the price may not either. What will drive the growth? How is the competition?

4. There are always more companies. It's hard to be patient in an age when stock quotes can be delivered to cell phones. But lots of companies can be researched and may show better growth rates.

5. Patient investors are rewarded. Most investors make money on stocks they don't sell; that is, they hold them, reinvest dividends, and buy at lower prices. Human nature dictates the opposite, however. Impatient investors buy and sell when a company is doing well, buy more when it's not going anywhere, and hold on to losers. How do you avoid this trap? Do your research and do it thoroughly. Be your own devil's advocate. Is this a company you could hold for the next ten years?

6. What are the negative aspects impacting the company and its industry? Is the profit margin changing? Why? What are the goals of the company? If it's in a slump, how does management plan to revise goals? What key products and services are going to drive growth?

KITCHEN-TABLE TIP

WHY IT'S BEST NOT TO BAIL

There will be bear stock markets. That's a fact of life. Should you attempt to leave the market if you think it's turned south? Since 1956, there have been nine downturns of 20% or more, which are the standard definitions of bear markets. That's once every five years. Let's say you got out of stocks in the early 1970s, which was a dismal time for stocks as inflation raged in the aftermath of the Vietnam War. After hitting a low in 1974, the market rebounded handsomely, producing a 14.6% annual average return during the next twenty-year period. Had you stayed in the market, you would have doubled your money.

More Long-Term Strategies

Part of the idea of investing is that capitalism shares its profits, but only if you make some sort of commitment. That means taking risk over a period of time, reinvesting the dividend, and doing the work to monitor your companies to see that they are consistently making money. If you've managed to save enough money to invest, why not make it a decades-long commitment? Do you get married with the idea of leaving your mate in a few hours? Do you buy a car and keep it for one month? Do you buy a refrigerator, stove, dishwasher, and furnace thinking that you'll need a new one next year? I know these are apples-and-oranges comparisons, but think of it: Why should investing in companies entail a short-term strategy? Why not invest in trends that are certain to happen? Can you take an overall strategy to something as volatile as the stock market? Especially when it takes 500-point swings in a day? To keep your sanity—and reinforce a long-term perspective—keep in mind a few certainties about life, society, and human mortality:

The HAT (Health, Aging, and Technology) approach to investing embraces companies that cater to all or some of the above certainties. You can pick stocks that employ these themes or mutual funds that target industries or segments of industries. If you're going to build and balance a portfolio, and you cover these avenues of human activity, you (or your club) will fare well over the next thirty years.

How to Stay the Course

Investing is really a matter of rational faith. You know that if companies keep producing earnings, their stock prices will go up and you will make money, too. Shorter term, you know that if you buy government bonds or leave your money idling in a money market fund, it will be there when you need it. But what happens if cataclysm roils the markets and you start to lose faith?

Like the seasons, the markets are cyclical, but when it comes to behavioral economics, nobody is ever sure when the seasons are changing. Should you pull your money out of the stock market when chaos rules? Is the best place for your money a government bond when interest rates are tormenting stock investors? The best advice is counterintuitive. Just stay put. That's right. Leave your money in the market if you're investing long term and keep it in the parking places I mentioned in chapter 4 if you need your money in less than five years for a major purchase(s).

Actually, the most nerve-preserving advice I can give are things you should not do:

- Don't watch CNBC, financial news shows, or monitor the market every second on the Internet. What happens second to second or even month to month won't make a difference if your money is invested for decades.
- Don't watch the performance of indexes. Even if you are invested in a stock index mutual fund, what counts is year-to-year performance. In any given twenty-year period (at least in most of the twentieth century), stocks have made money more than 90% of the time. But you have to stay invested in the market to achieve those gains. The technology-heavy NASDAQ index, for example, was getting creamed in April of 2000, meaning anything from computer hardware to wireless communications stocks were down from 14% to 29%. That sounds awful at first blush, but over ten-year periods, these stocks were still the top performers by huge margins.
- Most people guess wrong about the market. This is a consistent fact about human nature. Investors who think they know when the market will turn typically either sell out when the market has a long way to go on the upside or don't sell when the market is in a steep decline. In other words, most investors guess wrong most of the time and miss out on profits. Unless the economy is in a recession, and the stocks you've invested in have no earnings, it's best to stay where you are.
- Want to improve your returns in the stock market? Buy and hold. Households that traded frequently achieved annual returns of 11.4%, according to the American Association of Individual Investors. But those who traded less than average earned better returns—an average 16.4%.

- If you invest in long-term trends, you will be guaranteed some profits. Referring again to my HAT strategy (from chapter 6) your profits will be guaranteed if you bet on companies that make medicine or medical technology, cater to the aging population, or produce technology that saves the global economy money and time. You don't even need to understand what these companies do to make money. Just pick a few leaders or invest in stock index mutual funds.

Accepting Risk and Sleeping at Night

Investing involves some risk. So does walking down the street, getting in your car, eating bad food, and getting on a carnival ride. Unlike a long list of dangerous activities, there are far more rewards to be gained from investing than possible negative outcomes. It's a matter of screening the risks and taking a long view. If you can reasonably guess at where a handful of companies are headed—given all of the factors that you can measure with public information—you've done everything you could to be an informed investor. It's uninformed investors who buy on tips, fads, or hunches who get burned. Even if your portfolio has only three winners out of five, the gains of the leaders will more than make up for the slugs.

So you don't have to "beat the market" to be a successful investor or even match the average of the market. You probably won't anyway. It's like Aesop's tale of the tortoise and the hare. The hare was distracted and overconfident. The tortoise won largely because of his consistency and his ability to look down the path and concentrate on his goal.

How do you stay the course and avoid the myriad distractions? Look at the total return of your portfolio once a year, preferably at tax time. If you're beating the inflation rate, you're on your way. As I write this, inflation has been under 4%, so you don't have to do a whole lot. Certainly 8% is a no-brainer and 10% is achievable in an index fund. If you want to boost returns, consider one of my "wild card" mutual funds and put no more than 25% of your money in it. There will be more risk involved in these funds, but it won't put your nest egg in peril. As with stocks, if you can find a long-term performer and won't be distracted by a bad year, then hold on to it.

There have been bear markets in which it's a bad time to invest in stocks. They have happened only twice in my lifetime. These markets are characterized by two huge factors:

1. Inflation is rising at a double-digit clip and is out of control. This devalues stocks because investors jump into bonds to grab ever rising yields. Interest rates rise, real estate prices are inflated, and everything costs more while people are making less in real dollars. A late '70s, early '80s bear market is certainly possible, but not likely if the rise in the consumer price index is under 5% a year. In short, stocks thrive when interest rates and inflation are under control. If that's no longer the case, your best bet is government bonds and real estate.

2. Wages are out of control. When wages chase ever-rising prices stocks tumble even more, since the costs of doing business can't be controlled or predicted from year to year. That devastates profits and depresses stock prices. One popular theory about the West's most recent business expansion cycle is that wages have been kept at bay due to technology gains and improvements in productivity. This explanation doesn't always hold water in my opinion. A lot of high-paying manufacturing jobs have gone to third world countries that are conveniently devoid of unions, pension plans, overtime, health care, and environmental laws. That keeps the cost of production down and doubles profits. The consumer gains, but for how long?

If either #1 or #2 change for the worse, stick to your money market fund and government bonds. If they don't change, stay in stocks. Basically, follow Will Rogers's dictum: "Only buy stocks if they go up; if they don't go up, don't buy 'em."

Fine-Tuning Your Club and Its Portfolio: When to Sell Stocks

You can always dump stocks from your portfolio, but you need to abide by a few criteria and give the stock at least a year before you make a decision to sell. Every company is hostage to market cycles, industry downturns, market swings, or simply being ignored by Wall Street. You can sell a perfectly good company simply because Wall Street is bored by it.

Earnings always drive a company's growth, but profits can be eroded by short-term events. Companies buy and sell other companies, accounting mistakes are made, and they often acquire losing businesses. Well-managed companies admit their mistakes, take the "earnings hit" and suffer the resulting stock-price dip. Then they move in and figure out what they need to do. When Motorola discovered it had goofed big-time on digital cell phones (they bet on the wrong standard), they lost market share, their stock price dived, and Wall Street trashed the company. Then they recovered and restructured the company. The stock price climbed from a low of $48 to $178 in under two years.

Some companies really don't get it because they are run by unimaginative dullards. In this regard, it helps if top executives are paid in stock options. They personally suffer when the company is badly managed. How do you spot the laggards?

- **Companies blame outside forces for their problems and don't enact management solutions.** I know this sounds like something from a management textbook, but it's true. Quality managers admit their woes, make corrections, and move to bolster profits. They announce what they do and they do it. Dump do-nothing companies, but give them at least a year for the benefit of a doubt.
- **Companies blame the economy for their problems.** If a recession strikes, this is certainly a valid excuse. When the economy turns down, people buy fewer "durables" like homes, cars, and appliances. That's a legitimate excuse for some companies, but not those in businesses that are providing essential products and services.

Food, drugs, utilities, and any company involved in fixing or replacing things will thrive. Technology, automakers, and commodity producers (paper, petrochemicals, etc.) will suffer. You can always reposition your portfolio to "recession-proof," it with stocks that thrive in bad times.

▪ **Companies go through a rough patch.** Even good companies make mistakes. They acquire stinker companies or businesses that are overvalued. Case in point: Quaker Oats bought Snapple for way too much money and the business promptly took a nosedive. Quaker Oats is an old, reliable food company. Snapple hit its peak of popularity just before it was sold. This happens. Good companies figure out what they need to do in terms of shedding unprofitable assets. If they don't, you should sell—but again, give them a year to do it. The truth is slow in arriving to most corporate headquarters.

▪ **Companies fall out of favor.** There is a long list of these companies, but you should hold on to their stock, because the market is like a pendulum. A good example is RPM, a coatings company that makes Rust-Oleum, which has increased profits every quarter for more than thirty years. Its stock price has done nothing in the last two years. Is it a bad company? No. It's working through some internal problems, but it's otherwise profitable. It makes sense to hold on to languid companies if the profits are still there.

FIVE THINGS TO IGNORE ON THE WAY TO BECOMING A SUCCESSFUL INVESTOR

1. **Hot tips.** I've found that most hot tips are designed to enrich the person touting them and are rarely researched or present good long-term investments.
2. **Selling when a company is doing well.** Your goal as an investor is to reinvest and compound your profits, not enrich a broker. If you've done your homework, keep on investing. The stock will split and you can buy more shares.
3. **Taking risks.** We all take risks crossing the street, driving to work, getting in and out of the bathtub, eating greasy foods.

The stock market is the least-risky investment vehicle long term. You're putting more money at risk when you play the lottery, in fact, you're nearly always guaranteed to lose it.

4. **Professional advice.** While a heart surgeon can reasonably predict how a bypass operation will go and a lawyer can reasonably predict how an estate plan will avoid taxes, no "professional" is good at predicting or timing the stock market. If you learn about stocks and do your research, you will be guided by facts, not promises.

5. **You don't know anything about it, so you won't learn.** I'm always amazed at people's capacity for convincing themselves that they can't learn. But many of us have been brainwashed to believe this horrible lie. We can learn at any age at any time at very little cost. The information is free and the knowledge is priceless.

SUMMARY

1. Understand that investing is a matter of faith, but you can know the risk factors.
2. Don't try to time the market. Stay put.
3. Look at your investments once a year.
4. Sell stocks or funds only if your companies aren't making money or the economy is producing rampant inflation.
5. Keep on learning and investing.

CHAPTER 10

Autopilot Investing: Making Your Kitchen-Table Plan Work Automatically

There is no wealth but life. Life, including all its powers of love, of joy, and of admiration. That country is richest which nourishes the greatest number of noble and happy human beings; that man is richest who, having perfected the functions of his own life to the utmost, has also the widest helpful influence, both personal, and by means of his possessions, over the lives of others.
—John Ruskin, *Unto This Last*

If you're going to take some risks while investing, why not go for as much growth as you can stomach? You can be more conservative in your company retirement plans. With your own portfolio—and that of your club's—you can take as much risk as possible because you don't have as much invested. I believe that's the tack taken by the ABC Investment Club, which was one of the top clubs in the Midwest last year. (The ABC Investment Club [not its real name] has done so well that its members were concerned about their privacy. So I've renamed the club and changed the name of its president to Beatrice King.)

Beatrice King says that the twenty-dollar-a-month dues go into a high-risk portfolio of mostly technology stocks. Their portfolio looks like a growth mutual fund, not a ladies' investment club whose members average fifty-five years—many are retired. In business since 1983, Bea said their penchant for technology shares is taken because "that's where the money is."

Their portfolio is a who's who of technology leaders over the past five years. The software giant Microsoft is there, as is the computer-networking goliath Cisco Systems. Industrial companies are represented as well in Harley-Davidson and Modine. There are even a few medical technology companies in Medtronics, which makes pacemakers and Safeskin Inc., a medical products company. They have done the math on every company, estimating where the high price might be in the next five years, the possible low price and the

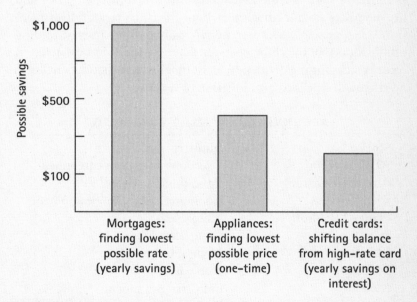

START SAVING NOW ON BIG-TICKET ITEMS

The first example shows how much you can save on a $100,000 mortgage (30-year/fixed rate) if you can get the lowest rate available. When shopping for appliances, you can save up to $100 per purchase by finding the lowest price. If you have at least a $2,000 balance on your credit card, you can shift the balance to lower-rate cards and save up to $130 per year in interest charges.

price ranges. They have fully employed NAIC's *Stock Selection Guide* (see chapter 6 for more information) to build a portfolio that is zeroed in on earnings growth.

The growth-oriented strategy has paid off, with the ABC portfolio appreciating some $17,000 in one year alone. The statement they supplied showed a total portfolio value of more than $63,000, which grew from a total investment of just $8,785.20. Not only do they show spectacular gains, they started early. They bought Microsoft in 1993 and have been buying technology stocks ever since.

"Our investment club is for growth; we don't really care about dividends," Bea remarks of the club's goal. On her own, Bea has transformed her own portfolio of 100% U.S. Treasuries into a growth stock portfolio, which has "helped in retirement."

Since the club is their seedbed for investment learning, Bea said her members are not concerned about the club's lack of diversification. They manage their own portfolios in a different way, feeding off the ideas that the club generates. Many of the members invest in utility stocks for the dividends; all of them realize that they will still need growth stocks to beat inflation over time.

ABC INVESTMENT CLUB PORTFOLIO

Stock	Industry
ADC Telecom	Telecommunications equipment
Advantage Learning	Educational software
Cisco Systems	Computer networking equipment
Harley-Davidson	Motorcycles
Intel	Computer chips
Medtronics	Medical technology
Microsoft	Software
Modine	Industrial equipment
Paychex	Payroll processing
Safeskin	Medical
Solectron	Technology

Saving and Growing Automatically

No matter how old you are or where you are in life—as exemplified by the ABC club—you still need growth in your portfolio. Once you've done the research, those growth stocks split. You buy more at lower prices and reinvest the dividends. The math is simple and compelling, as you have seen. There is another aspect of growth that has nothing to do with money. It is an awareness that you grow with your investments, that you stop being a consumer and start producing the kind of ideas that will sustain you the rest of your life. To do that, you need to acknowledge that you are not just a consumer, but a *grower*.

Author Laura Sewall beautifully observes that "we mistake consumerism, the endless acquisition of things, for the saving of our lost souls; we bury our lost sensuality in the thin guise of rationalism ad nauseam; and we limit truth to right and wrong." Even though we can acquire the knowledge to increase our wealth, there are other, deeper life issues to consider. You are saving and investing money to give you the time and flexibility to pursue what's important in life.

In this book I hope to center your life on saving money. There is, however, another aspect of saving that impacts your personal ecology: When you save money you are saving *yourself.* If you work to make money, you are conducting an exchange. You exchange your life energy for currency. So money is not only symbolic of what you did to earn it, it's active and stored energy, like radiant heat from the sun or chemical energy from your muscles. It's no surprise that the language of money and energy is much the same. We spend money. We expend energy. Currency is money. Current is electricity. So when we save money, it's as if we have created a battery of our life energy. It is stored until we need it to do the business of our life.

Of course, we need money to spend on the details of life, but if that's the only way we see that relationship, we're headed for trouble. Much of our culture is directed toward spending money for status, acquisition, and false images. This spending blinds us to the fact that by spending it exclusively on material things, it blinds us to our own mortality and suffering. We need to reinforce behaviors that focus on saving our life energy.

We can use our money to relieve our pain—and the pain of others—but it won't eliminate our suffering. I came across this passage that Pope John Paul II wrote in 1995 in his *Evangelium Vitae*. It struck me that he had more insight into our fractured relationship with money than most economists, politicians, and social critics combined. I've condensed, edited, and italicized the passage a bit, but it points to how we have mistaken materialism for what we really need in life:

> The eclipse of the sense of God and of man inevitably leads to a practical materialism, which breeds individualism, utilitarianism, and hedonism . . . The values of *being* are replaced by those of *having*. The only goal that counts is the pursuit of one's own material well-being. The so-called quality of life is interpreted primarily or exclusively as economic efficiency, inordinate consumerism, physical beauty and pleasure, to the neglect of the more profound dimensions—interpersonal, spiritual, and religious—of existence.

The pope's larger point, I believe, is that we've become slaves to materialism and it's spiritually *impoverished* us. While I can't discount his spiritual message, I can suggest there's also a secular message here as well. Our obsession with money for money's sake has devalued our relationships with each other. We work more and more hours to pay for more and more things: bigger houses, bigger vehicles, bigger boats, etc. That takes us away from our families, depriving them of our *being*. Even if we have bad relationships with our family and communities, the fact that we are there with them is often the most important thing we can contribute. I often think my best hours of existence are spent with my daughter and wife just sitting together. No TV. No radio. No videos. Just sitting and being together. We don't have to spend a dollar to do it and it's a spiritual comfort that is priceless.

And then there's the "quality of life" issue. How can we possibly have a decent life if we are working all the time and worrying about money? We are all diminished if we live to work and spend. That's not a culture of freedom, that's a culture of slavery to some consumeristic ethic. We are social creatures and demand meaningful interaction. We need to nurture each other, learn from each other, and even drive each other crazy sometimes. That's how we grow. It's only by conserving our life energy that we can save precious pieces of our lives for others. Saving money is one way that catalyzes our energy into family/community growth. It's sound personal ecology because our energy goes back into the wider "ecosystem" that is our family, neighborhood, community, county, state, country, and society. We replenish the rest of the world if we can save our life energy. Instead of depleting self and the resources around us, we "give back" to nurture those around us. It's a cycle and it starts with self-conservation.

How Millionaires Save Themselves

My friend Chuck Carlson, whose books on dividend reinvestment and wealth building are classics, did a survey last year of millionaires. Those who were in this league were staunch savers, of course, but they did other things that contributed to their ability to save, namely:

- They stayed married an average of thirty-two years. Divorce is really expensive.
- They held on to the same job for a long time. Job-hoppers have trouble building wealth.
- They have invested over their working careers—an average of thirty years.
- They had no investment experience when they started—85% knew zilch—but learned as they went along.
- They considered themselves "frugal." Some 80% saved by not spending.
- They held investments for more than five years.
- They used their parents as models for saving and investing.

It's easy to be distracted in your relationships with others and to money. If you focus on growing yourself and your money (in that order), over time you'll discover that you won't even care about money anymore and other truths and joys become automatic. But first, you have to turn off the distractions and listen to the Tibetan spiritual master Sonyal Rinpoche when he observes:

> Modern society seems to me a celebration of all of the things that lead away from the truth, make truth hard to live for, and discourage people from even believing it exists. And to think all of this springs from a civilization that claims to adore life, but actually starves it of any real meaning; that endlessly speaks of making people "happy," but in fact blocks their way to the real source of joy.

In order for us to find our sources of joy (money is only a means of helping us find it), we need to examine the language of saving and see how we can learn to speak it better. Money is not the center of our lives any more than flowers are the center of a butterfly's. To establish a sound personal ecology with money, we need to learn how to talk to ourselves, to save the words that are meaningful to us and allow us to save ourselves. Of course, this may be too abstract of an approach with money, but my larger point is that saving our life energy is the main goal. That is why putting money aside each month to invest is so important; it frees us up to do other, more life-giving things. If you're still stymied by my philosophy, the box below shows a few more concrete ideas for saving:

KITCHEN-TABLE TIP

25 MORE WAYS TO AUTOMATICALLY SAVE FOR INVESTMENTS

1. Ask your credit card company to waive its annual fee. The credit card business is so competitive that a decent bank will do this. Pay off your balances when you get the card.
2. Bring your lunch to work at least twice a week. Put your savings into your investment club or money market fund.

3. Buy your home or car at the end of the year. Bank the savings.
4. Buy floor-model appliances. Skip the extended warranty.
5. Buy private-label brands at the supermarket. Skip convenience foods. Grow your own.
6. Check to see which magazines you don't read and cable channels you don't watch. Cancel what you don't use. Write a check to your money market account.
7. Always audit your property tax bill. There may be some huge mistakes on your assessment that could save you hundreds—perhaps thousands of dollars.
8. Obtain higher savings yields and lower loan rates at a credit union.
9. Save on entertainment by checking out free events sponsored by your local parks, libraries, or schools.
10. Take advantage of senior or children's discounts.
11. Save on college expenses by getting your children's prerequisites out of the way at a local community college.
12. Never shop hungry and avoid products displayed at eye level. They cost more.
13. Don't shop by the price tag in the supermarket, shop using unit price by volume. That's how you get the best deal.
14. Save money on airfare by avoiding travel in peak season or on Friday and Monday evenings, when premium fares are in effect.
15. Buy airline tickets at least 21 days in advance, consider alternative airports and staying over Saturday night. You could save up to two-thirds on your fare.
16. Review your insurance coverage on everything you own. Raise deductibles to save money.
17. Shop for money-saving offers on the Internet, see: www.coolsavings.com, www.dotdeals.com, www.ecoupons.com, www.specialoffers.com.
18. Use your air conditioner sparingly. If in a hot climate, buy a unit with a 12 SEER rating or better.
19. Replace all of your incandescent lightbulbs with compact fluorescents and save up to 10% on your electric bill.

20. Tune up your furnace every year by cleaning it. Replace filters once a month.

21. When buying a vehicle, never pay "document" fees or buy "credit life insurance" or extended warranties.

22. Never start negotiating from the sticker price; start with the "invoice price" (available from *Consumers Digest* magazine or www.consumersdigest.com). You can even negotiate on major appliances. Give it a try. There's lot of competition out there for your dollar. Walk away if you don't get the deal you want.

23. Know what your trade-in is worth and stick close to its book value. See www.kbb.com for an estimated value.

24. Track your monthly expenses with greater precision. Buy Quicken or Microsoft Money.

25. Always ask for a discount in fees or rates from your bank if you do direct deposit of paychecks or automatic debits of mortgage payments.

The Language of Saving: How to Translate

I marvel at the power of language in describing what we can do. We save, conserve, and nurture so that all of us can grow. We are living things in living systems. Paper currency is not alive, but it symbolizes life in its most potent form. As paper, it was once alive. It is up to us restore life to it and infuse those around us with its potential energy. Buying things we don't need surrounds us with nonliving things that will never grow, never be enriched by our presence. If we can limit our acquisitions to the things that sustain us, that's a start. We can be simple in our pleasures and nurturing in our pursuits. To that end, I have some ideas that will coincidentally also help save you money.

- **If you don't know how, learn how to entertain yourself.** This applies to your entire community. While I certainly see nothing wrong with going to see a concert or movie now and again, there is much virtue in self-entertainment, and it's becoming a lost art. As the novelist Reynolds Price once sighed in a National Public Radio commentary, "I'm afraid we've lost the ability to amuse ourselves." Of course, you can download music from the Internet, jog with earphones, and buy hundreds of thousands of CDs, DVDs, videos, and audiotapes. We are blessed with a culture that embraces nearly every form of music, visual art, dance, and literature. You can learn about these things in the public library, cultural centers, local colleges, and it won't cost you much of anything. You can buy a used guitar at a thrift shop for a few dollars. You can bang on a tambourine. You don't have to be a musician to make music. I was trained as a musician (violin, guitar, piano, French horn) and was a professional playing weddings and parties. Now I'm studying to be a competent amateur. I have to learn how to do it for the love of it. It doesn't cost me anything. I have stopped buying CDs. I want to hear the music that only I can make. You can too, and save the thousands you may spend on recorded music, stereo equipment, DVD players, big-screen TVs, and anything related to "canned" music. Make your own movies. Record your own songs. Write your own books. Anybody can dance. Anybody can create their own art. You don't have to do it for money. It will fill you up. It will replenish your energy. It is yours and you won't have to pay somebody else to amuse you.

▪ **Make things yourself.** All you have to do is look at early America and you can discover all the things we used to make ourselves and how rewarding it was. There's an "old village" in every state, although it goes by different names. In Virginia, it's Williamsburg. In Illinois, it's New Salem. In California, it's *not* Disneyland. Every village like these living museums used to produce food, candles, clothing, furniture, building supplies, leather goods, shoes, and hundreds of other items that are manufactured in some other part of the world. Of course, for most of us it would be impossible to make our own minivans or DVD players, but that doesn't mean we can't make our own clothes, food, and craft items. Not only can we save money on some of these items, but we can make them better and save a tremendous amount of money. Kathleen makes my daughter Sarah's Halloween costume every year. Sarah has the most unique, nonlicensed costume of all of her friends. My mother has been making Sarah's Christmas dresses. I write songs for Sarah customized to her favorite tank engines. We all take joy in what we make—and we save money in doing it. Can you bake your own bread, desserts, and pastries?

I know, who has the time? But if we make the conscious decision to make the time, our energy will flow back to us. It's an interesting cycle, but it works. It's not surprising that you can acquire (buy or rent) nearly any tool to make or fix whatever you want. Work by hand saves us and "localizes our labor." That means, instead of exploiting women and children in a third world sweatshop to make some branded clothing item, we make it *ourselves* and our money/energy flows back to us in a direct benefit. Instead of buying a $4 greeting card for every holiday, birthday, and anniversary, we make them ourselves with our personal message. It's more intimate. Instead of a spendfest with shopping lists, holidays become a personal exchange of life energy. These are hardly radical ideas, and I'm not the first to suggest them. But in the context of saving money by making things ourselves, we save ourselves for others.

- **Grow your own and stop complaining about food quality.** Everyone can grow food, even if you live in an apartment. Cities have community gardens. You can even rent space for a garden in suburban areas. When you grow your own food, you control what goes into it. Want real organic produce without paying through the nose? Go get some composted manure and do some "integrated pest management." Hundreds of books have been written about it and it's not hard to grow things without pesticides and artificial fertilizers. You can even make your own compost with grass clippings, kitchen scraps, and leaves in your own composter. Better yet, can or freeze what you grow and save it for those dark winter days. There are hundreds of seed catalogs, thousands of garden shops and books on gardening. Why complain about what goes into processed foods when you can make a safe and wholesome product yourself? Do you have any idea how much your health will benefit and how much money you'll save?

- **Vacation at home.** You matter how many deals or travel packages you see advertised, they are still expensive relative to traveling close to home or just staying home. I'm not opposed to that occasional overseas trip or relaxing cruise, it's the "mandatory" vacation that becomes wasteful. For some reason, affluent Americans have it ingrained in their heads that they *have* to go out of town in spring and summer. Whether it's Walt Disney World at spring break or France in August, it's costing a fortune. When I visited Europe in my late twenties, it was by rail and staying in youth hostels and cheap hotels. Now trips are priced in thousand-dollar increments, even domestic ones. If you consistently plan these trips twice a year, that's several thousand dollars out of pocket for a week or two that will involve 1) a hassle in and out of airports; 2) bad meals and lousy service; and 3) pictures you'll probably never look at again.

So why not stay home and save money for your New Prosperity? Name any metropolitan area, and I can list at least three things that can cheaply occupy you for a week. There are museums, zoos, cultural centers, central cities, and hundreds of things to do that cost very little. Just pick up the newspaper or scan a local Web site. In the summer, there are county fairs, carnivals, festivals, and concerts. In Chicago alone, there are world-class jazz, blues, and gospel festivals, ethnic fairs—and they're all free and you can take the train to get there. *Every* city and county has something to offer. You will not only save money getting there, you'll sleep in your own bed that night, pack your own meals, and enjoy the place in which you live. Where I live now, I can walk or bike ride to the county fair, a farmers' market, a community center, a college, a golf driving range/golf course, a beach, a playground, a horse barn, a prairie preserve, a commuter train station, a supermarket, library, soccer field/basketball court, and bike trails. I have to find a very good reason these days to go to that marvelous madhouse known as Chicago O'Hare International Airport. Staying home saves you money, energy, and nerves.

▪ **Walk around, shop locally.** You will see things more clearly if you just take a walk around your neighborhood, your town/city center and your community at large. Don't take my word for anything on how to save your life energy and your money. Do it yourself by just poking your head into storefronts. Nearly everything you need to know is in your public library. Support your local businesses. Concentrate on short trips, and your ability to spend money will be reduced. If you don't have to drive to the mall, you won't be tempted to buy anything there. If you walk to the local fruit stand, you won't load up on expensive processed convenience foods. Is it that simple? No, but it's the beginning of a savings ethic. You save your personal time in shopping alone and you'll save money.

By walking around your community, you'll discover the "secondary economy." That means used clothes, furniture, books, and tools. Nearly every town center has at least one thrift shop, usually one that benefits a charity. We not only donate all of our old clothing and furniture to our thrift shop, we patronize them. By any measure, new things are incredibly overpriced relative to workable used items. That's because they're made on other continents, shipped at great expense, and advertised at even greater cost. Used merchandise is already waiting for us in every community. Instead of sending our money/life energy overseas to exploit abused and underpaid workforces, our energy is rechanneled into our own communities. As Naomi Klein observes in *No Logo: Taking Aim at the Brand Bullies* (Picador, 1999), the process of shipping production overseas and closing community manufacturing of goods means that "the people doing the work of production are likely to be treated like detritus—the stuff left behind."

We can reverse that trend, however, and improve human rights abroad and in our own communities. Save money by eschewing new branded goods and shop locally. My favorite thrift shop benefits a crisis pregnancy center. A coworker volunteers her time at a thrift shop that benefits a home where her mentally disabled son resides. My wife shops at a store that benefits a hospital. So your dollars go back into the community and help your neighbors—and yourself. But you won't find these places off the interstate at the outlet complex or at the mall. You have to walk around your community, if for no other reason than to see what's there. I've discovered that I can walk to get a great haircut for $11 from my barber, Abe; buy used books and fresh produce; go to Walgreen's and buy anything from batteries to toothpaste (our club owns the stock); I can walk to Jeremy's Hot and Delicious, the local hot-dog place; a paint store; a church; a shoe repair shop; and a restaurant-pub. Each dollar you spend at a local business goes back to a family in the community. Your town collects money on permits and retail taxes so it can buy fire engines, fix sewers, and keep your streets clean without raising taxes. Save your gas, save your community, *save yourself.*

Why Save? We Can't Take It with Us!

If you're buried with money, it'll only become more fertilizer for the cemetery lawn and trees. You can harness money's power by saving it now. Even the free radiation from the sun is useless unless we can convert it to bioenergy through plants or electricity through solar panels, which is then stored in batteries at night. We save because it contains our essence and we can use it later. You spend it today, you won't have it tomorrow when you want to buy that house, send your children to college, and retire. There is a power to money, but that energy will not produce happiness or immortality by itself. We have to transact some other business in our life to make that happen. The best way to deal with money is to make the process of saving it virtually invisible yet efficient—like a conduit buried within our lives.

Because an unquestionable life force is contained in our money, it makes our lives more meaningful when we learn how to conserve it for maximum growth. We hope to grow with our money and our life energy thrives and touches other lives when this happens. As a result we become more whole, more balanced with our inner and outer needs, and are able to achieve a sound personal ecology.

Growing with money, learning how to save and invest, and even learning how to spend it are not taught with a sense of balance in our modern culture. Perhaps we should teach money management and *gardening* at the same time. Or learn money management and *music* at the same time. Each art requires attention to balance. There is an element of fertilization, germination, and flowering to money. It's also true that there's a tempo, volume, tonality, and harmony to how money may be balanced. It can be shrill or harmonious depending on how we save, spend, and invest. Whatever we do, we need to make sure that money serves us. The simplest way to regard money is like a tiny voice that encourages you to do the right thing, like Jiminy Cricket in *Pinocchio*. When we listen to this little chirping—and abide by it—our lives will be a lot more fulfilling than wishing upon a star.

HOW TO MAKE YOUR SAVINGS AUTOMATIC: A SUMMARY

1. Know where you stand with your money and personal ecology. Are you saving enough for your and your family's future?
2. How can you save in terms of big ticket items like housing, transportation, and debt? Start a savings plan based on reduced spending and long-term savings.
3. What vehicles do you have for basic savings receptacles? Set up money funds as staging areas and short-term holding places for your money.
4. How can you save and invest through investment clubs or on your own? Start up a club, even if you do it by yourself.
5. Pick stocks yourself for growth. Hold them long term and reinvest dividends at low cost.
6. Pick mutual funds for growth. Keep it simple. You only need four to "own" nearly the entire world of stocks.
7. Know what you need to do to diversify your portfolio and lower risks. Combine money market funds, government bonds, stocks, and mutual funds.

8. Know that the market and home equity long term will grow for you, and even cyclical downturns will be short-lived.
9. Prepare yourself for the future by learning how to make good investment decisions and sell off bad investments.
10. Money is energy. Know how to conserve it, tap it, and spread it around. Enjoy it.

Resources

Online Brokers: Why Pay More?

The online brokerage business is one of the most competitive sectors of the financial services industry. It's a great example of how the marketplace lowers prices to meet demand. Every mainline brokerage house now has an online counterpart that offers competitive commissions. Even the pure "cyberbrokers," with no branch offices, are providing a great deal of service at commissions brokers would have laughed at five years ago.

As a result of the intense competition, commissions have plummeted. A survey by the American Association of Individual Investors (AAII) found that in early 2000, average minimum commissions fell to $18 with nearly half of the seventy-six firms surveyed offering commissions below $15. Compare that to $50 for a discount broker or $75 for a full-commission broker and you can save a tremendous amount of money on trades—money that can be invested instead of diminishing your total return on invested capital.

Even more notable about the commission war is that flat rates are offering even better deals versus the percentage-based commissions of traditional brokerages. The AAII found that seventy out of the seventy-six online brokers surveyed offered a flat-rate schedule.

Although their research is of limited value, most online brokerage sites offer news, quote services, earnings estimates, and the ability to track the value of your portfolio—free. The better sites will even allow you to chart or screen stocks you are following. You can also talk to "live" brokers and tie in your account to a "cash management account" that also offers a money market account, credit card, statements, and other financial services.

The greatest drawback of online brokers is that the computer systems backing them up may go down, meaning your trade won't go through at the price you wanted. As with any broker you deal with, "fulfillment" of the trade is important, so you need a written or e-mail transaction of every trade. There's also the temptation to trade more, make bad decisions, and buy and sell without any discipline. Online trading should be transacted only after you've done your research and plan to stay invested for the long term.

Following is just a sampling of the universe of hundreds of online brokers. Surf around until you find the broker with the lowest commissions and best services.

Accutrade, www.accutrade.com

AF Trader, www.aftrader.com

American Express, www.americanexpress.com/trade

Ameritrade, www.ameritrade.com

Bank of America, www.bankofamerica.com/investments

Brown & Co., www.brownco.com

Bull & Bear, www.bullbear.com

Burke, Christensen & Lewis, www.bclnet.com

Datek Online, www.datek.com

Donaldson, Lufkin & Jenrette, www.dljdirect.com

E*Trade, www.etrade.com

Fidelity, www.fidelity.com

FirstTrade, www.firstrade.com

Investrade, www.investrade.com

Morgan Stanley Dean Witter, www.online.msdw.com

Mr. Stock, www.mrstock.com

Muriel Siebert, www.siebertnet.com

MyDiscountBroker, www.mydiscountbroker.com

Net Investor, www.netinvestor.com

Quick & Reilly, www.quick-reilly.com

Schwab, www.schwab.com

Scottsdale Securities, www.scottrade.com

Scudder, www.scudder.com

Strong, www.estrong.com

SureTrade, www.suretrade.com

T. Rowe Price, www.troweprice.com

Trading Direct, www.tradingdirect.com

Waterhouse, www.tdwaterhouse.com

Wingspan, www.wingspan.com

Your Discount Broker, www.ydb.com

Top Financial/Investing Web Sites

Better Investing/NAIC, www.better-investing.org. If you're starting out, or just looking for a few decent stocks to buy at low cost, this is the first place to visit. Sponsored by the National Association of Investors Corporation, this nonprofit group is the heart and soul of amateur investing. The site provides links to investment clubs and lots of advice.

CBSMarketwatch.com., www.cbsmarketwatch.com. A treasure trove of personal finance information, once you get past the screaming market-oriented headlines.

Gomez Advisors, www.gomez.com. Although not specifically a financial site, the Gomez group evaluates and rates financial Web sites that offer brokerage and banking services on costs, ease of use, and overall utility. A really useful site that could save you a lot of time.

Morningstar, www.morningstar.com. In addition to good reporting on mutual funds and stocks, this site offers portfolio monitoring, news and "Quicktake" reports on stocks and funds.

Quicken, www.quicken.com. You'll find everything from useful financial calculators to mutual fund picks. A great place to start for all kinds of information on personal finance issues, loans, insurance, and financial management.

Smart Money, www.smartmoney.com. One of the best of the sites, tied into a publication that features online calculators, articles, and portfolio planning.

Great Government/Nonprofit Web Sites and Toll-Free Numbers

Alliance for Investor Education, www.investoreducation.org. An omnibus site that focuses on basic education skills and investor protection. A highlight is the "Kid's Savings Calculator" that shows how small amounts add up over time.

American Savings Education Council, www.asec.org. The best feature of this small site is the "Ballpark Estimate" calculator that gives you a thumbnail prediction of whether you're saving enough for retirement. Also features basic savings strategies.

College Savings Plan Network, www.collegesavings.org. Sponsored by the National Association of State Treasurers, a great resource on college savings planning and descriptions of state programs.

Consumer Information Center, www.pueblo.gsa.gov. A cornucopia of free government information on everything from pensions to Social Security.

Credit Union National Association, www.cuna.org. As the main trade group behind credit unions, this organization can locate a low-cost credit union near you and provide advice on getting low-interest loans for mortgages and vehicles.

Health Care Financing Administration/Medicare, www.hcfa.gov/medicare. A complete guide to Medicare benefits and ratings of nursing homes that receive federal financing.

Internal Revenue Service, www.irs.ustreas.gov. The mother lode of tax forms and publications.

Investing Online Resource Center, www.investingonline.org. Jointly sponsored by the Washington State securities agency and Investor Protection Trust, an excellent primer and resource on online investing and brokers.

Investors Protection Trust, www.investorprotection.org. Sponsored largely by state securities regulators, a site on basic investment information that will allow you to check broker backgrounds, avoid scams, and plan for retirement.

Library of Congress, thomas.loc.gov. A one-stop site for federal government information and other federal Web sites. (You can also check for nearly any book in print.)

Money2000, www.money2000.org. A purely educational site that provides useful background on saving, spending, debt reduction, and investing. Also features debt-reduction calculators and great links.

National Association of Insurance Commissioners, 816-842-3600. You can check on the background of financial advisers who sell insurance. Also check the National Association of Insurance and Financial Advisers, 202-331-6001.

National Association of Securities Dealers, www.nasdr.com, 800-289-9999. This quasi-government agency partially regulates securities dealers. You can check the background of your broker, learn about securities fraud and warnings from the National Fraud Information Center, or obtain basic rules governing stockbrokers.

National Foundation for Consumer Credit, www.nfcc.org, 800-388-2227. This organization's specialty is credit counseling. They operate "Neighborhood Financial Care Centers" with counselors who will craft a plan to get you out of debt.

National Fraud Exchange, 800-822-0416. Do you think you've been offered an investment that sounds like a scam? For a small fee, you can check it out with this service and be on the safe side.

North American Securities Administrators Association, 888-846-2722. An easy way to check on the background of any securities dealer or broker.

Pension Benefit Guaranty Agency, www.pbgc.gov. The place to start for anything concerning defined-benefit pension plans or locating lost defined-benefit pensions.

U.S. Department of Energy, www.doe.gov. Check out fuel-efficiency ratings on vehicles and how to save money on home heating bills.

U.S. Department of Housing & Urban Development, www.hud.gov. A guide to buying your first home, which includes the HUD Home-buyer's Kit.

U.S. Department of Labor, Pension and Welfare Benefits Administration, www.dol.gov/dol/pwba. A useful source for publications on retirement and how to monitor your pension plan's investments from the agency that polices fund managers.

U.S. Securities & Exchange Commission, www.sec.gov, 800-732-0330. The main entry point to the SEC's EDGAR database of filings by public companies. An invaluable resource for stock investors. Also check out www.edgar.stern.nyu.edu/mutual.html for SEC filings by mutual funds. Another useful subsection of the SEC site is their mutual fund cost calculator, which helps you compare the costs of similar mutual funds over time. You can also check broker backgrounds through the toll-free number.

U.S. Small Business Administration, www.sba.gov. A fine resource guide on starting your own business that includes links to small business counselors and education.

U.S. Department of the Treasury, www.ustreas.gov. An indispensable source for everything concerning Treasury and savings bonds. Click on the section called Bureau of Public Debt or go directly to www.publicdebt.treas.gov/sav/sav.htm.

U.S. House of Representatives, www.house.gov. A useful site for member information, committee assignments, and e-mail addresses.

U.S. Senate, www.senate.gov. The Senate's Web site.

Veterans Administration, www.va.gov. If you are a veteran, find out what benefits you qualify for.

Commercial Sites

Although these sites prompt you to buy products or services, they contain a number of links, useful pieces of information, and software. The sites make their money from advertising, membership, or usage fees.

Accuquote, www.accuquote.com, 800-442-9899. An efficient way of quoting life insurance policies and calculating how much coverage you need.

America Online, www.aol.com, 800-827-6364. The nation's largest Internet access provider/online membership service has a host of financial resources.

American Association of Individual Investors, www.aaii.com. Although run by a nonprofit membership organization, in order to gain full use of this excellent site you need to be a member of AAII.

AltaVista Money, www.money.altavista.com. This subsection of the popular search engine combines news, stock quotes, portfolio management, and the message boards (on specific stocks) from ragingbull.com.

Bank Rate Monitor, www.bankrate.com. A primary source for the best rates on certificates of deposit, credit cards, and mortgages nationwide. There are also some useful articles on personal finance and debt management.

bivio, bivio.com. Gives investment club information.

Bloomberg, www.quote.bloomberg.com. While not the most complete of sites, Bloomberg provides a total-return calculator for mutual funds.

CarsDirect, www.carsdirect.com. You can buy vehicles directly through this site.

CBSMarketwatch, www.cbsmarketwatch.com. Although focused on financial and investing news, this comprehensive site has excellent coverage of mutual funds, personal finance, and anything relating to investment.

Compuserve, www.compuserve.com, 800-848-8199. Like America Online, a major Internet access provider and source of investment information.

Dealernet, www.dealernet.com. A referral and quote service for more than 7,000 auto dealers across the country.

Deloitte & Touche, www.dtonline.com. A handy resource on taxes, financial planning, and retirement issues.

E-Loan, www.eloan.com. If you feel comfortable with getting a loan online, this is the place to start.

Fidelity Mutual Funds, www.fidelity.com. Although a big billboard for hundreds of Fidelity products, check out their retirement planning software.

Finance Center/Smartcalc, www.financenter.com. Easily one of the most practical financial calculators on the Internet. You can estimate everything from car payments to retirement savings.

401K Café, www.401kafe.com/tools/calc.html. A unique calculator that lets you project how much your 401(k) will be worth over time. Lets you plug in factors like salary growth, pension contributions, and inflation.

GE Financial Network, www.gefn.com. The company that makes lightbulbs, appliances, and generators also offers mortgages, insurance, and mutual funds.

Get Smart, www.getsmart.com. Credit card information.

Gomez Advisors, www.gomezadvisors.com. A leading site that rates the quality and usability of other investment Web sites.

HSH Associates, www.hsh.com. The best mortgage rates in the United States.

IBC Financial Data, www.ibcdata.com. The first place to check for the best returns on money market mutual funds and bond funds. Also see www.imoneynet.com.

Insurance Corner, www.insurancecorner.com. A master site for consumer information on insurance agents and news.

Insure Market, www.insuremarket.com. As part of the Quicken site, Insure Market will quote and link you to a variety of insurance products.

Insurance Web, www.insweb.com. Another source for insurance policy quotes and information.

Intellichoice, www.intellichoice.com. A good tool for researching the total costs of vehicle ownership.

Intelliquote, www.intelliquote.com, 888-622-0925. A quote service and calculator for life, health, and auto insurance.

IOwn.com, www.iown.com. A comprehensive real estate site that will allow you to search for homes, prices, and mortgages.

INVESTools, www.investools.com. Information on stocks, mutual funds, and portfolio management software.

Invest-o-rama, www.investorama.com. Provides links to more than 2,000 investment-related sites. A good source for investment clubbers.

JD Power, www.jdpower.com. Consumer rating firm evaluates everything from cars to online brokerage Web sites.

Keynote Systems, www.keynote.com. Another rater of online brokerages.

Leasesource, www.leasesource.com. A good source for vehicle leasing deals that can show you whether it's cheaper to lease or buy.

Lifenet, www.lifenet.com. Mortgage calculators and worksheets.

Loansdirect, www.loansdirect.com. A quick way to obtain online lending.

Mortgagebot, www.mortgagebot.com. A search engine for mortgages and related services.

Mortgage Maze, www.maze.com. Mortgage qualifying calculator and credit information; order credit reports online.

Morningstar, www.morningstar.com. One of the most engaging and useful sites on the Web, includes profiles of stocks and mutual funds. One of the best features is an online portfolio monitoring program that will automatically store and update values on all of your stock and bond holdings. Also includes financial news and columns.

The Motley Fool, www.fool.com. While oriented a little too much toward their own merchandise, this site is chock-full of basic investment tips and portfolios for novice and intermediate investors.

MSN Money Central, moneycentral.msn.com. A treasure trove of useful articles and calculators that will help you do everything from get out of debt to save for retirement.

NetstockDirect, www.netstockdirect.com. A well-designed site to access a program for direct stock purchase and dividend-reinvestment plans.

Networth, www.networth.galt.com. Fund information and portfolio tracking program.

PCFN, www.pcfn.com. Run by a securities brokerage, a good source for stock quotes, charts, research, and news from Reuters, Business Wire, and PR News, all searchable. You can even build portfolios online.

Prodigy, www.prodigy.com, 800-776-3449. The smallest of the "Big Three" (with America Online and Compuserve), Prodigy has several investment resources.

Quicken, www.quicken.com. An omnibus site that allows you to track ten portfolios, obtain stock quotes, track the top-performing mutual funds, and much more.

Quickquote, www.quickquote.com. A service for life, health, and annuity quotes.

Quotesmith, www.quotesmith.com. This site will quote a variety of low-cost insurance products from term life to long-term care.

RAM Research, www.ramresearch.com. A primary source to find the best deals on any type of credit card.

Scott Burns, www.scottburns.com. Some down-to-earth personal finance columns from the syndicated investment columnist.

Standard & Poor's Personal Wealth, www.personalwealth.com. An investor's tool that provides everything from stock reports to portfolio management.

Strong Funds, www.strong-funds.com. Provides basic investment/retirement information in its educational section.

TheStreet.com, www.thestreet.com. Although the prime focus of this hyperactive site are today's market movers, there are smaller sections on mutual funds and personal finance. Features columnists Herb Greenberg and James Cramer.

Thomson Investors Network, www.thomsoninvest.net. A subscription service that provides information and analysis on stocks, bonds, and mutual funds.

T. Rowe Price, www.troweprice.com. The best retirement planning software on the Internet. Also provides a good college-planning kit.

Quote.com, www.quote.com. Electronic mail stock-quote and alert service.

Charles Schwab, www.schwab.com. An omnibus site that includes everything from a college savings calculator to free charting of stocks. Delayed stock quotes also available.

The Vanguard Group, www.vanguard.com. This site features a host of online calculators and a mutual fund cost calculator that shows you how much more money you can earn by investing in a low-cost mutual fund.

Wall Street City, www.wallstreetcity.com. A subscription service that tracks stocks, bonds, mutual funds, indexes, and futures.

Yahoo, www.finance.yahoo.com. A subsection of the search engine that provides thousands of links to financial sites of every stripe.

Financial Planning Referral Organizations

Looking for a financial planner who can help you chart out everything from estate plans to taxes? These referral services will help you find a qualified financial planner in your area. Be sure to ask for references, how they are compensated, and what services they provide.

American Institute of Personal Financial Advisers, 800-862-4272. A branch of the American Institute of Certified Public Accountants that specializes in financial planning. These certified public accountants do everything from financial plans to tax preparation.

Certified Financial Planner Board of Standards, 888-237-6275. Want to find out if a certified financial planner (CFP) has been sanctioned for illicit financial-planning practices? This service will do background checks on CFPs who have earned that designation.

National Association of Personal Financial Advisers, www.napfa.org, 888-333-6659. This group represents "fee-only" planners who will charge you for their time instead of commissions on products they sell. They are a good first choice if you need a planner, since they don't have an inherent conflict of interest in recommending products that earn a commission.

Financial Planning Association, www.fpanet.org, 800-282-7526. One of the largest trade groups representing planners of every stripe; also provides local referrals.

Society of Financial Service Professionals, 888-777-7077. This group can refer you to Chartered Financial Consultants (ChFCs) and Certified Life Underwriters (CLUs). Although these professionals are mostly insurance agents, they can prepare financial plans.

Search Engines/Information Sources

These services are pure information retrievers, pulling all sorts of things from cyberspace, phone books, and beyond. Most search engines combine free e-mail with the ability to search the Web, message boards, and e-mail news.

AltaVista, www.altavista.com. One of the most comprehensive search engines available.

Dogpile, www.dogpile.com. A multisearch engine that will search many engines at once; spotty but interesting.

Excite, www.excite.com. A search engine hybrid that offers Yellow Pages listings, stock quotes, maps, newsgroups, and e-mail lookups. Not as good as Infoseek or AltaVista, though.

Google, www.google.com. An interesting search engine.

Hoover's Online, www.hoovers.com. Company financial profiles and links to other sites. Also available on America Online.

Hotbot, www.hotbot.com. A snappy search engine, linked to *Wired* magazine.

Infoseek, www.infoseek.com. A diverse hybrid that combining indexing, search engines, and other gateways to Yellow Pages and e-mail lookups.

Looksmart, www.looksmart.com. A combination search engine/index, this versatile site is powered by the venerable AltaVista search engine, but also features "personalized" lists of magazines, news services, and local sites.

Lycos, www.lycos.com. Your basic search engine with all the features offered by the competition.

Newslink, www.newslink.org. Links to more than 3,000 publication-sponsored sites; sponsored by the *American Journalism Review.*

NorthernLight, www.northernlight.com. A useful indexing and search engine that can find obscure sites that other engines may miss.

QuikPages, www.quikpage.com. A national directory of business Web sites.

SavvySearch, www.savvysearch.com. Like Dogpile, this site will perform metasearches of several search engines.

Yahoo, www.yahoo.com. Relying more on lists of indexes, Yahoo is all things to all people in cyberspace.

Media Sites

Although offering limited information, these sites are good places for background information on nearly any financial topic.

***Barron's* Online, www.barrons.com.** The weekly Dow Jones investment magazine features stock and fund information.

***Better Investing,* www.better-investing.org.** *Better Investing* is the magazine of the National Association of Investment Corporation (NAIC), the nonprofit mother organization of stock investment clubs. You'll find a plethora of advice on investment clubbing, picking stocks, and links to hundreds of clubs across the United States.

Bloomberg Business News, www.bloomberg.com. News on companies and portfolio management software.

Business Week **Online, www.businessweek.com.** Online feature of the business magazine, loaded with portfolio tools, research capability, and links to online banking across the country.

Business Wire, www.businesswire.com. Company press releases and news.

Consumer Reports **Online, www.consumereports.org.** The searchable version of the magazine available on a subscription basis.

CNN, www.cnn.com. Headlines from the Cable News Network and CNNFN, CNN's Financial News channel.

Edmunds.com, www.edmunds.com. A spin-off of the specialty auto magazines, a good source for vehicle reviews, pricing, and specs.

Financial Times, **www.ft.com.** Online version of the international financial newspaper. Good for global financial news.

FortuneInvestor, www.fortune.com. A spin-off from the magazine, loaded with portfolio tools and research.

Money Magazine, **www.money.com.** A bountiful source of articles, calculators, and investment picks.

MSNBC, www.msnbc.com. Briefs from the cable network's news coverage; also includes NBC News items.

New York Times, **www.nytimes.com.** Lead stories from the national newspaper. Also on America Online.

Reuters News Service, www.reuters.com. Hot stories from the Reuters wire service.

USA Today, **www.usatoday.com.** A quirky but searchable site.

Wall Street Journal, **www.wsj.com.** An abbreviated version of the financial newspaper. For the full, searchable version, you pay a subscription fee.

Washington Post, **www.washingtonpost.com.** A generous site that includes archived stories from the *Post*'s fine personal finance columnists including Jane Bryant Quinn. Its most valuable feature, however, is the ability to search the Associated Press newswires.

The Whiz, www.thewhiz.com. Owned by the same company that publishes the Bank Rate Monitor Web site, this is an excellent site for younger investors.

Worth Magazine, www.worth.com. The Web site is actually better than the magazine, which is owned by Fidelity Investments. Features include "Ask Peter Lynch," message boards, and useful financial links.

Miscellaneous Consumer/Shopping

These sites will help you save money on any number of consumer products.

American Civil Liberties Union, www.aclu.org. Information on using the courts and government accountability.

Amazon.com, www.amazon.com. The premier online retailer of books, videos, CDs, drugs, tools, and toys. Also offers online auctions.

Auction Octopus, www.auctionoctopus.com. This unique site is a search engine for other auction sites.

Autosite, www.autosite.com. A vehicle pricing and buying service.

Barnes & Noble, www.barnesandnoble.com. The bookseller also sells music, videos, and out-of-print books.

Borders Books, www.borders.com. Although not as complete as Amazon or Barnes & Noble, Borders offers a good selection of books and music.

Buy.com, www.buy.com. A major site for discounted consumer items.

Buyers Edge, www.buyersedge.com. A site that will price and sell you thousands of consumer products.

Cars.com, www.cars.com. A comprehensive site that will not only price new and used cars, but locate the vehicles and local dealers.

Carsmart, www.carsmart.com. Vehicle pricing service with links to dealers and manufacturers featuring invoice prices.

Consumers Digest, www.consumersdigest.com. Brief reviews of a wide range of consumer products from autos to household goods.

ConsumerWorld, www.consumerworld.org. If you go no other place on the Web for consumer information, try this site. Its 1,500 links are incomparable; everything from the best deals in credit cards to a "Private Eye" section for locating people, products, and information.

CCSNY, www.ccsny.org/weblinks. Essential links to consumer groups, credit information, and government information.

Ebay, www.ebay.com. One of the largest online auctioneers of tens of thousands of products from every category.

Equifax, www.equifax.com. Information on credit reports.

Essential Information, www.esssential.org. The master site that will link you to most of the Nader-founded consumer groups, including the Center for Auto Safety, Center for Insurance Research, Center for Science in the Public Interest, Center for Public Integrity, Coalition for Consumer Health and Safety, and Public Citizen.

E-town, www.e-town.com. Reviews of home electronics products.

Etoys, www.etoys.com. A source for discounted toys and fun stuff.

Experian, www.experian.com. Information from the credit bureau service formerly called TRW.

GTE Superpages, www.gte.net. A master site for searches of White and Yellow Pages, classified ads, employment ads, and business Web sites.

H&R Block, www.hrblock.com. As you can guess, a site devoted to tax advice and tax-preparation software.

Investment Company Institute, www.ici.org. Sponsored by the trade group for the mutual fund industry, this site features updated news on legislation and subjects impacting investors.

Kelley Blue Book, www.kbb.com. The premier source for vehicle prices, used and new.

Mutual Fund Education Alliance, www.mfea.com. The mutual fund trade group features a retirement worksheet.

Mutual Funds Interactive, www.fundsinteractive.com. News and discussion on mutual-fund topics based on www.quicken.com.

National Association of Enrolled Agents, www.naea.org. The latest tax news and information on income taxes and filing tips.

Parent Soup, www.parentsoup.com. Reviews of baby products, videos, and software.

PC World, **www.pcworld.com.** Reviews of computers and peripherals.

Popular Mechanics, **www.popularmechanics.com.** Reviews on vehicles and electronics and articles on home improvement topics.

Product Reviews, www.productreviewnet.com. Reviews on thousands of appliances, vehicles, computers, and health and beauty items.

Productopia, www.productopia.com. A site selling a number of consumer items, such as appliances and electronics.

Realtor.com, www.realtor.com. Sponsored by the largest real estate trade group (National Association of Realtors), this site is an excellent way of pricing and locating homes in any area of the country. It includes maps, neighborhood information, and broker links.

Travel

Airlines.com, www.airlines.com. One-stop shopping to find all of the airline Web sites, which are the first destinations for finding specials and low fares, especially if you are in frequent-flyer programs. Also see www.smilinjack.com.

American Society of Travel Agents, www.astanet.com, 800-965-ASTA. Locate a travel agent by zip code and specialty plus access information on travel tips, warnings, and consumer protection.

Expedia, www.expedia.com. Microsoft's mega-site will book anything from airline flights to rental cars and provide extensive information on any travel topic.

Travelocity, www.travelocity.com. It's a toss-up as to which site offers more, but like Expedia, Travelocity has an excellent airfare search engine and a host of travel information.

Trip.com, www.trip.com. Another service that will help you plan nearly every aspect of your vacation.

Notes

Preface

Mother Teresa, as quoted in *The Quotable Soul* (Wiley, 1996), edited by Claudia Setzer, p. 106. An excellent place to start before you deal with money matters.

Henryk Skolimowski, *Ecophilosophy* (Boyars, 1981), p. 33. An eminently sensible way in which to view the world and its relationship to the human economy.

Chapter 1: Introduction: A New Prosperity Begins at the Kitchen Table

John Muir, *The Wilderness World of John Muir* (Houghton-Mifflin, 1954), p. 319. Another fine place to start if you need to understand your relationship to the world.

Peter Montague, "The Lottery," *Rachel's Environment & Health Weekly* 646, 15 April 1999, www.rachel.org. Although Montague usually writes about environmental and economic topics, I spotted this gem on lotteries while looking for something else.

Associated Press, "Market Collapse," 15 April 2000. The stock market was plummeting as I was researching and writing this book. It recovered while I was editing it, a great example of what stocks do over time.

John Ruskin, *Unto This Last* (Appleton-Century Crofts, 1964), p. 109. A classic treatise from the nineteenth-century sage on the importance of money and labor. I stumbled upon these superb essays while reading Mohandas Ghandi, who said Ruskin was a major influence.

Paul Tillich, *The Courage to Be* (Yale University Press, 1952). An inspirational read from the great theologian.

Employment Benefit Research Institute, *1999 Retirement Income Confidence Survey,* www.ebri.com. This important annual survey highlights major trends in retirement. EBRI was the main source for my research on the need for retirement savings in this chapter.

Chapter 2: Found Money: How to Find the Money to Invest

Abdullah Yusuf Ali, *The Meaning of the Holy Qur'an* (Oman Publishing, 1996), a beautiful and informative interpretation of the holy work. Forgive my interpretation of this quotation.

TV-Free Campaign literature, www.tvfree.org. If you want to know the relationship between the tube and the relentless advertising it rams into your home, this is the group that is battling the medium.

Robert Samuelson, *Washington Post,* www.washingtonpost.com. Mr. Samuelson is one of our most honest and premier interpreters of the link between politics and the economy.

Marc Eisenson and Nancy Castleman, *The Banker's Secret* (Good Advice Press, 1997). The authors are inspirational savers whose book and software by the same name can save you thousands on your mortgage and other daily expenses.

Joanne Ciulla, *The Working Life* (Times Books, 2000), p. 200. One of the most definitive examinations of working, labor, and the economy you'll ever read.

Bill McKibben, "Joys 'R Us: What Could Be More Fun Than Materialism?" *Utne Reader Online,* 13 April 2000. A fun piece on Gandhi, modern life, and the economy.

Arne Naess, *Ecology, Community and Lifestyle* (Cambridge University Press, 1989), translated by David Rothenberg, p. 88. A hearty introduction to "deep ecology" by the renowned Norwegian philosopher.

Jim Motavalli, "Sprawling America," *E Magazine,* May/June 2000, p. 4. A short piece on transportation costs in the environmental magazine.

Amy Carr, "Top 10 Reasons to Love $2 a Gallon Gasoline," *Daily Herald,* Arlington Heights, Illinois, 16 March 2000. Amy did the math on what it costs to fill up a beastly SUV versus a subcompact and how it adds up real fast.

Quicken.com calculators. For this chapter, I used the online calculators extensively at www.quicken.com to compute the various savings over time.

Not only is the math done for you to see how saving small amounts adds up, you can see what it grows to if you invest it over several decades' time.

Chapter 3: Creating Your Own Investment Club

Voltaire, quoted in *The Oxford Book of Money* (Oxford University Press, 1995). A fine book of anecdotes and quotes on money and economic matters.

The National Association of Investors Corporation, Madison Heights, Michigan. There is no better source on investment clubbing than the NAIC. Check out their fine Web sites at www.better-investing.com and www.naicmedia.com.

Also see www.investorama.com.

Linda Kelly, *Two Incomes and Still Broke? It's Not How Much You Make, It's How Much You Keep* (Times Books, 1996). A fine compendium of ways to save money using simple worksheets.

Chapter 4: Parking That Pays:
Great Savings Places for Your New Prosperity Funds

Lionel Trilling, from "Art and Fortune," as condensed from the *Oxford Book of Money.*

Edward Abbey, "Crying in the Wilderness," *Notes From the Secret Journal,* (St. Martin's Press, 1989), p. 89. A collection of rants and epigrams from the great western writer.

Government Web sites: www.ustreas.gov and www.ssa.gov. The main online resources for the U.S. Treasury Department and the U.S. Social Security Administration will tell you anything you want to know about government bonds and Social Security, respectively.

Brooke Stephens, *Wealth Happens One Day at a Time* (HarperCollins, 1999). If you need a daily approach to saving, this is a good place to start.

Chapter 5: Creating Your Kitchen-Table Pension Plan

www.dol.gov/pwba. A fairly complete description of all the different types of tax-deferred retirement plans can be found on this U.S. Department of Labor Web site, which also contains some useful links and ways to save money.

www.vanguard.com, the Web site of the Vanguard Mutual Fund Group, contains great research on index mutual funds, and mutual fund cost and after-tax return cost calculators.

Chapter 6: Long-Haulers: Stocks to Buy and Hold

Ralph Waldo Emerson, *Wealth* (Library of America, 1983). A timeless essay from one of our greatest philosophers.

Ken Janke and Thomas O'Hara, *Starting and Running a Profitable Investment Club* (Times Books, 1998). In addition to my own *The Investment Club Book* (Warner, 1995), an essential volume on stock investing and clubs.

Richard Ferri, *Serious Money: Straight Talk About Investing for Retirement* (Portfolio Solutions, 1999), p. 133. Although not the best written investment book, it's loaded with useful information.

Chapter 7: A Regular Reward:
Reinvesting Dividends and Buying More Shares

The Oxford Book of Money, edited by Kevin Jackson (Oxford University Press, 1995), 191 p. 419.

Charles Carlson, interview. Read anything by Chuck and you'll know everything there is to know about dividend-reinvestment plans and direct-investment plans. I recommend his *Buying Stocks Without a Broker* (McGraw-Hill, 1996) or his Web site, www.dripinvestor.com.

Jane Bryant Quinn, "Hold On to Your Stocks," *The Washington Post,* May 4, 2000. Nuts and bolts facts about why long-term investing in the stock market is a great idea.

Chapter 8: The Million Dollar Portfolio:
Supplementing Your Nest Egg with Mutual Funds

Jonathan Clements, "Criticisms of Indexing Don't Hold Up," *Wall Street Journal,* 25 April 2000. A summary of why index funds are a perfect investment for most people, by the writer of the "Getting Going" *WSJ* column.

For more background on mutual fund investing, consult my *Late-Start Investor: The Better-Late-Than-Never Guide to Realizing Your Retirement Dreams* (Owl/Henry Holt, 1999).

Chapter 9: Fine-Tuning Your Kitchen-Table Plan:
How to Stay the Course and Know When to Sell

Jacob Needleman, as quoted in *Money, Money, Money: The Search for Wealth and the Pursuit of Happiness* by Michael Toms (New Dimensions, 1998).

"How to Prepare Your Portfolio to Bear a Bear Market," in *The Vanguard*, Spring 2000. Some encouraging facts about staying the course in down markets.

Chapter 10: Autopilot Investing:
Making Your Kitchen-Table Plan Work Automatically

John Ruskin, *Unto This Last* (Oxford University Press, 1923), p. 109. I return to Mr. Ruskin's wisdom.

Laura Sewall, *Sight and Sensibility: The Ecopsychology of Perception* (Tarcher, 1999), p. 132. An extraordinary book on perception. I'm not sure how it relates to money, but I saw things differently after reading it.

Diane Rosener, "The ABCs of Saving," as cited in *The Pocket Change Investor*, P.O. Box 78, Elizaville, NY 12523. A fine little missive on basic savings.

Charles Carlson, *Seven Steps to Seven Figures* (Random House, 2000). Chuck surveyed and interviewed millionaires to see how they made their money. A must-read.

"Smart Ways to Save More Cash," *Your Money*, June–July 2000, p. 76. A primer on automatic ways to save in the nation's premier personal finance magazine.

Pope John Paul II, www.vatican.org. I excerpted this section from a larger work. Pope John Paul II is a trenchant observer of materialism.

Sogyal Rinpoche, *The Tibetan Book of Living and Dying* (Harper-SanFrancisco, 1992). A classic treatise on life and death.

Index